*Bc*

# WINNING FOOTBALL
# WITH THE
# MULTIPLE WISHBONE

Glenn Carson

Parker Publishing Company, Inc.

West Nyack, New York

© 1981 *by*

Parker Publishing Company, Inc.
West Nyack, New York

**Library of Congress Cataloging in Publication Data**

Carson, Glenn
  Winning football with the multiple wishbone.

  Includes index.
  1. Football—Offense. 2. Football coaching.
I. Title
GV951.8.C37    796.332′2    80-26727
ISBN 0-13-960922-9

Printed in the United States of America

# *What This Book Will Do For You*

The Wishbone offense is one of the most effective offenses in football at both the high school and college levels. Wishbone teams have had among the highest winning percentages in college football during recent football seasons, but defenses have a way of catching up with offenses in the cycle of football. Defenses have already started to become more effective against the basic Wishbone. Therefore, multiple attack variations are needed to support the effectiveness of the basic Wishbone offense. This book presents the basic Wishbone plus changes and variations to keep the offense ahead of the defense.

The philosophy of the basic Wishbone is given for both the flow side, counter flow and passing attack. The philosophy behind the complementary offense, power series, outside veer series, sprint out series, flip-flop offense, special plays and multiple formations is given.

Organizing the Wishbone base is explained. Organizational basics are the huddle, break, alignment and spacing, numbering system, stance, snap count, play series, numbering defenses and blocking system. Defenses are recognized and numbered for ease in carrying out assignments. A combination blocking system is provided so that the offense can take advantage of blocking angles.

The basic Wishbone running attack is thoroughly explained and it includes both the flow and counter flow offense. The flow offense consists of the fullback veer, belly, option, and triple option. The counter flow offense consists of the quarterback counter, counter dive and counter option.

The Wishbone has established itself as one of the greatest rushing offenses in the history of football. This book stresses the rushing offense and also shows you how the Wishbone can reach its potential as a passing offense. A simple and very effective passing attack is included that blends in with the running offense. The various pass routes and good pass protection are described. The basic passing attack includes the tight end hot pass, the cross pass against both three- and four-deep defenses, the divide pass, the veer bootleg pass, the veer keep pass and a quick screen pass to the split end. Several individual split end routes are shown.

You may want to run the triple option but because of personnel limitations, especially at quarterback, may be reluctant to install the triple option in the offense. There are several ways to disguise what you are running and give the opposition the triple option appearance. Several different plays may be predetermined and run with triple option blocking. Blocking patterns may be changed. These concealed plays have all the appearance of the triple option but are easier to execute. This makes the quarterback's job easier but still keeps the pressure of the triple option on the defense.

Almost any type of play can be run from the Wishbone alignment. Some Wishbone coaches say that you do not have a Wishbone play if the quarterback does not step out and first mesh with the fullback who runs a course over the guard's outside foot. The Wishbone of the future will have to expand from the basic plays and include reverses, end-arounds, quarterback keeps, quick pitches, crossbucks, traps, cutbacks, draws, screens and running passes. All these complementary plays to the Wishbone base are included in this book.

One big reason for success in coaching is adapting your offense to your personnel. This book offers other offensive plays to supplement the basic attack. These plays can be used according to the players' talents. They can also be used to take advantage of the opponent's defense and various game situations. The multiple Wishbone has the advantage of not having to change offensive alignments from year to year. Keep the same offensive alignment but change the offensive plays to fit your personnel's abilities.

A complete power series of plays is included. This forces the defense to defend against the quickness of one-on-one blocking and against power double-team blocking at the same time. This is really the best of two worlds; one-on-one quick blocking and double-team isolation power blocking. The power plays can be the run-to-daylight type or predetermined to attack a specific hole. Counters and passes from the power run fake are also included.

Most teams using the Wishbone execute the inside veer triple option and all of its companion plays. The outside veer can also be used with great success from the Wishbone with minor adjustments. This opens a new dimension for the offense and greatly increases problems for the defense. Dives, options, counters and passes are included in the outside veer series.

The sprint out series is one of the best offensive series in football, and it can be executed from the Wishbone. This gives the running quarterback excellent opportunities to run. The sprint out series includes passes, screens, draws, sweeps, counters and reverses.

The flip-flop principle has several advantages and can be utilized within the Wishbone framework. A complete set of plays are included for the flip-flop Wishbone.

Special plays from the Wishbone and Broken Bone alignments are included. The selection and use of these plays are explained. Special plays that attack both inside and wide are given. These include dives, slants, crisscross, lead, and various types of option plays. Special draws, reverses, screens and passes are also included.

Wishbone coaches will have to consider many variations to add to their attacks in the future. The multiple Wishbone does this for you. Several Broken Bone formations including the double open, wing, flanker, pro, twins, slot, twins switch, twins open, strong, and combinations of these formations are shown. The use of motion by different backs from different positions is included. Shifting into and out of the Wishbone is shown. The unbalanced Wishbone and a half-spread are also described.

The successful coach must have a system for dealing with the clock. This includes how to use up time without incurring a penalty. The two-minute offense to conserve time is included, as well as a system of automatics and a no-huddle offense.

The multiple concept will be part of the Wishbone of the future. This book offers you the best of two worlds; the Wishbone in its basic, pure form and a wide open multiple Wishbone that enables you to use highly successful actions as reverses, end-arounds, keeps, quick pitches, crossbucks, traps, draws, screens, sprint outs, to add more power to the already potent basic Wishbone attack. Multiple Broken Bone formations, motion and unbalancing add to the total concept of the Wishbone of the future; THE MULTIPLE WISHBONE ATTACK.

                                        **Glenn Carson**

# CONTENTS

# WINNING FOOTBALL
## WITH THE
## MULTIPLE WISHBONE

# CHAPTER *1*

## *Understanding the Multiple Wishbone Offense*

The Wishbone was the catalyst for triple option football. Today it is not the only triple option offense but it is still widely used. The Wishbone offense has several advantages contained in its philosophy.

### THE WISHBONE BASE

The Wishbone can be run successfully with different types of personnel. Simplicity is a strong point of the basic Wishbone offense. The basic blocking assignments are simple. Most blocking is base straight ahead one-on-one blocking. The backs' play pattern or path routes on the basic plays are simple. The simplicity of the basic offense allows more practice time for fundamentals and drills. This added practice time will help make a football team stronger. Coaching is a fight against time. The simplicity of the Wishbone will save time.

The Wishbone is a mirrored offense that requires less depth because the third-best guard, tackle or halfback can be inserted to either side of the offense.

Since the Wishbone is balanced, the defense will probably be balanced. This is a great aid to the coach and quarterback in selecting plays to attack the defense. If the defense is unbalanced, it is easily spotted and attacked.

All basic plays start alike. The complete series of basic plays hits all along the lines of scrimmage and in the secondary on passes. The faking and deception are good on all the basic plays.

The basic Wishbone is a ball control offense. It is a goal line-to-goal line offense. No special plays or formation changes are required for any part of the football field. The Wishbone is a "hard nose" offense. Everyone plays football. Everyone hits and gets hit, including the quarterback. The "hard nose" aspect will make the team's defense tougher as they practice against the offense.

### Flow Side Offensive Philosophy

The flow side offense allows a fake inside and a lead blocker when running the option or triple option plays. The fullback takes the same path as the dive man over the outside foot of the guard on both sides of the offense. Fumble possibilities are lowered because of this. The offense can outnumber the defense. The assignment of the defensive men to stop the triple option will cut down on pursuit by the defense. This opens up the opportunity for other plays to be more successful.

### Counter Flow Offensive Philosophy

The counter flow offense is a very strong phase of the Wishbone because the defense has to be so concerned with the flow portion of the offense. While the defense is trying to stop the flow offense, the counter flow offense attacks quickly in the opposite direction. Long gainers can result because of this. The counter flow offense in the basic Wishbone hits quicker than in most offenses.

### Passing Philosophy

The great run threat of the Wishbone makes the passing game more effective. The quarterback has more time to throw and receivers are open more since the defense has to be so concerned with the run threat. Play action passes with the fake of the run help to accomplish this. The pass and the run must complement one another.

## THE SUPPLEMENTARY WISHBONE OFFENSE

The use of supplementary plays allows you to alter your offense from year to year to fit your personnel. This saves the time and effort of changing formations and systems. This is especially true if the multiple Wishbone is used. The Multiple Wishbone can be added to or changed to best attack the upcoming opponent from week to week. The Multiple Wishbone has enough variety to best utilize players' abilities.

### Complementary Wishbone Offensive Philosophy

Complementary Wishbone plays are picked out and used according to their need in certain situations. These situations are: long down and distance; certain defenses, to take advantage of a certain defensive man; time in the half or game; score; to take advantage of what the defense is looking for; taking advantage of your strengths and allowing the halfbacks to run all along the line of scrimmage. The time should never come when you do not have a play for any situation that presents itself in a game.

### Power Series Offensive Philosophy

The Wishbone alignment lends itself to the power series. The location of the backs for double-team isolation-type blocking is good. The balanced alignment does not tip off where the ball is going to be run. It is a simple series to install. The power series is good to use in bad weather and on wet, muddy fields. Good play action passes can be executed from the power series.

### Outside Veer Offensive Philosophy

Using the outside veer along with the inside veer in the Wishbone puts great pressure on the defense. The defense cannot use the same defensive responsibility assignments for both the outside and inside veer and remain sound. The outside veer is easy to install in the Wishbone and adds greatly to the multiple concept.

### Sprint Out Series Offensive Philosophy

Wishbone quarterbacks have running ability. The sprint out series gives the quarterback many opportunities to run. The option run pass and sprint out sweep are all designed to give the quarterback the opportunity to run. The sprint out series also gives the quarterback an opportunity to pass from a series in which he is focusing all his attention on reading the action of the defensive secondary. He cannot do this as well on play action passes. A complete series of plays can be run from the sprint out action.

### Flip-Flop Wishbone Offensive Philosophy

The flip-flop principle has several advantages. These advantages can be incorporated into the Wishbone. Play assignments are cut in half when using the flip-flop principle. Special player talents can be better utilized. The short slot set can give a stronger blocking front. Three quick receivers can release on passes. Motion can be utilized by the slot back and give several offensive formation variations.

### Special Wishbone Play Philosophy

Many special plays can be used with the Multiple Wishbone. Special plays should have a definite purpose and not be added just for the sake of having something different. They should be added to take advantage of the opponent's defense, to combat staleness of the offensive team, and to complement the basic plays of the offense. Special offensive talents can be utilized very well in special plays. The Multiple Wishbone offensive philosophy allows the coach many special play opportunities.

### Multiple Formation Offensive Philosophy

It is easy to go into various Broken Bone formations from the basic Wishbone. These formations put added pressure on the defense. The added possibilities of motion, shifting fron one formation to another, unbalancing the Wishbone and the use of spreads give the Multiple Wishbone coach unlimited offensive potential against his opponent. The Wishbone has been criticized as a poor "catch up" offense when you are behind in the score. The use of multiple Broken Bone formations and a more wide-open offense helps to solve this problem.

## THE TOTAL MULTIPLE WISHBONE PACKAGE

The Wishbone will become more varied and multiple in nature in the future. This is because smart defensive coaches will use new defensive schemes against the basic Wishbone. Individual defensive players will perform better against the basic Wishbone as they play against it more often and become more familiar with the execution of the basic Wishbone. The use of the Multiple Wishbone will keep the defense off balance with its varied looks and execution. The Multiple Wishbone coach now has the best of two worlds; the Wishbone in its basic, pure form and a wide-open multiple attack that is unlimited and can be as varied as the coach desires.

# CHAPTER 2

## Organizing the Wishbone Base

The simple basics that are sometimes taken for granted in football have to be organized and practiced to be effective. Executing the basics correctly will help insure that all other phases of the game will be executed correctly also. The basics needed to execute the offense are the huddle, break to the line of scrimmage, alignment and spacing, numbering system, stance, snap count, play series, defensive numbering and blocking system.

### HUDDLE

There are several types of huddles used to assemble the offense together to communicate between plays. Getting in and out of the huddle with ease and communication within the huddle are important. The center is responsible for setting the huddle. He must hustle from the previous play and set up five to six yards behind where the football will be placed to run the next play. He faces away from the ball. His hands are in the air so other players can see him. He also calls "Huddle, Huddle, Huddle" to let other players know where he is. The center sets only five to six yards from the ball because the huddle is reversed and closed to the defense so they cannot hear the play that is being called.

All other players hustle to align in the proper place in
relation to the center. The split end huddles just behind the
center. The guards will huddle on each side of the center. The
tackles will huddle one step in front of the guards and slightly
wider than the guards. The fullback and the tight end align
between the tackles. The halfbacks align one step in front of the
tackles. The quarterback steps into the opening between the
halfbacks to call the formation, play and snap count. He calls
the play only once. All players look at the quarterback to help in
communication. There is no talking in the huddle. The quarterback will get the play from a runner from the bench or a
signal from the bench before he steps into the huddle to call the
play (Diagram 2-1).

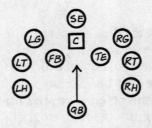

**Diagram 2-1**
**Huddle**

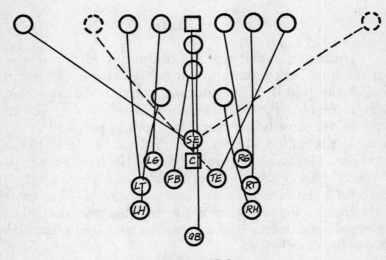

**Diagram 2-2**
**Huddle Break**

## BREAK

Sharpness in the huddle and a sharp hustling break to the line of scrimmage influence the defense, creating a mental impression that the offense is really geared up to attack the defense. After hearing the formation, play and snap count that is to be used for the next play, the offensive players all clap their hands and shout "Block." Then all the players sprint to the line of scrimmage to assume their alignment (Diagram 2-2).

## ALIGNMENT AND SPACING

Proper alignment and spacing are very important for successful offensive execution. Offensive plays cannot, and will not, be successful if the alignment and spacing are improper and sloppy. You must insist that alignment and spacing be exactly correct. The center is the first to align over the ball and all other players align accordingly. The guards have a constant three-foot split. The tackles have a three-to-four-foot split. The tight end has a three-to ten-foot split. The varying split of the tight end is important to put maximum pressure on the defense. The split end has a basic split of 12 yards. However he will not align closer than seven yards from the sideline. The ends flip-flop either right or left according to the formation that is called in the huddle (Diagram 2-3).

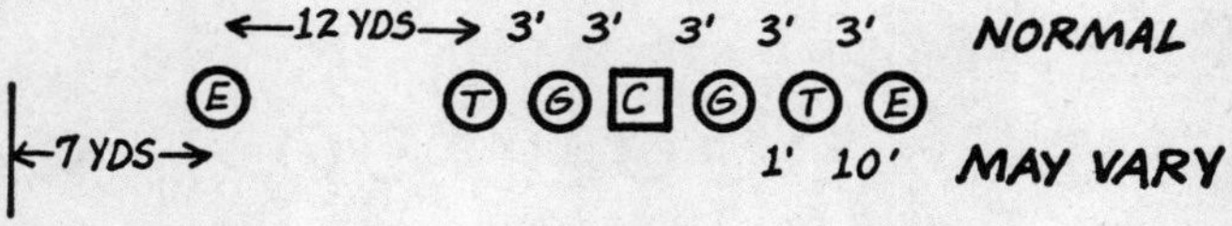

←12 YDS→　3'　3'　3'　3'　3'　　*NORMAL*

←7 YDS→　Ⓔ　　Ⓣ Ⓖ Ⓒ Ⓖ Ⓣ Ⓔ

　　　　　　　　　　　　1' 10'　*MAY VARY*

**Diagram 2-3**
**Line Alignment and Spacing**

The quarterback assumes his alignment just behind the center to receive the snap of the football. The fullback aligns his heels 13 feet from the front tip of the football. The fullback's alignment is important for timing on plays and as a guide for the halfbacks to align up on. The halfbacks align 15 feet from the front tip of the football. This means that the halfbacks are back two feet from the fullback and are aligned 18 inches to either side of the fullback (Diagram 2-4).

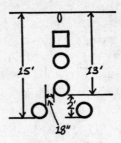

**Diagram 2-4**
**Backfield Alignment and Spacing**

## NUMBERING

The numbering system has the even numbers to the right and the odd numbers to the left. The center is the only man to have two numbers. The center's right foot is the zero hole and the left foot is the one hole. The right guard is number two, the right tackle number four and the right end number six. There is one additional hole wide outside the right end that is number eight. The left guard is number three, and the left tackle number five and the left end number seven. There is one additional hole wide outside the left end that is number nine (Diagram 2-5).

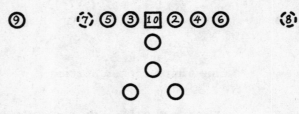

**Diagram 2-5**
**Offensive Hole Numbering**

## STANCE

All players align in a two-point stance except the center who is in a three-point stance, ready to snap the football. Offensive plays can be run from the two-point stance. The threat of plays being run from the "pre shift" or two-point stance will keep the defense off balance and prevent their charging so hard. It will also discourage defensive stunting and changing defensive alignments. The ball will be snapped on the first sound from the quarterback if the plays are run from the two-point stance. Otherwise, the first sound will be to put everyone down into a three- or four-point stance.

The split end uses a three-point stance with his inside foot back. He will turn his head toward the center to see the snap of the ball if crowd noise makes it impossible to hear the quarterback's snap count. The halfbacks also use a balanced three-point stance. The fullback and all linemen except the split end use four-point stances. Any pulling linemen must take some weight off their hands when they are going to pull. Otherwise, the linemen have enough weight on their hands to fire out straight ahead quickly.

## SNAP COUNT

Snap counts should be simple. Their aim is to get all the offensive players to move on the snap of the ball and get the jump on the defense. Snap counts should be designed for this first, and to fool the defense second. When all players are aligned on the ball in a two-point stance, the quarterback places his hands under the center to receive the ball. He is then ready to start the snap count. The first sound is "SET." If the football is to be snapped on "SET," the play will be run from a two-point stance. If the play is to be run from any other sound the players assume their three- or four-point stances on "SET." The football may be snapped on "SET," "HIKE" or "GO." The quarterback's complete cadence is "SET," "HIKE," "READY," "GO." The quarterback will draw out the "READY" with his voice ("READYEEE").

## PLAY SERIES

Every play is given a descriptive word or words to briefly describe the action of the play. The descriptive word is easier to remember than a number. A number is given to the play to tell where the ball will be run or faked. Diagram 2-6 shows the basic running plays, their descriptive terms and the hole number each play attacks.

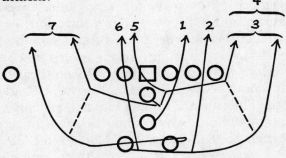

5. Sneak 1
6. Counter Dive 3
7. Counter Option 9

1. Veer 2
2. Belly 4
3. Option 8
4. Triple Option 8

**Diagram 2-6**
**Basic Running Play Description and Numbering**

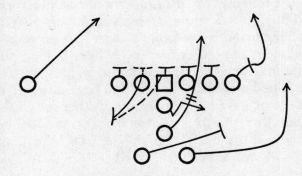

**Diagram 2-7**
**Veer 2 Hot Pass**

Passes also have descriptive terms and the running play fake that precedes the pass. Diagrams 2-7 through 2-11 show the basic passes, their descriptive terms and the running fake that precedes the pass.

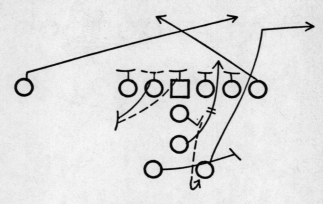

**Diagram 2-8**
**Veer 2 Cross Pass**

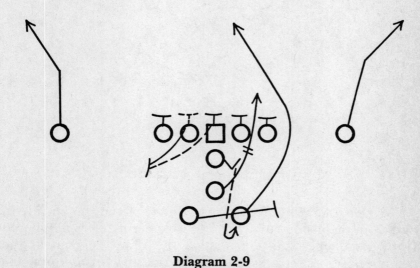

**Diagram 2-9**
**Veer 2 Divide Pass**

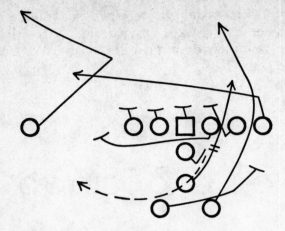

**Diagram 2-10**
**Veer 2 Bootleg Pass**

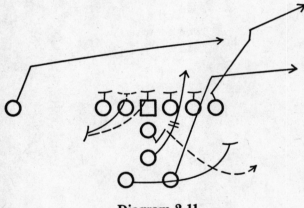

**Diagram 2-11**
**Veer 2 Keep Pass**

## NUMBERING DEFENSES

Defenses are numbered in two ways; from the outside in and from the inside out. The defensive perimeter is numbered from the deepest outside man as the first, the man in the contain position as the second, the man usually responsible for the quarterback on the option, the third, and the next man inside, the fourth (Diagram 2-12).

The defenses are also numbered from inside out. Any man over the center is zero. If there is no man aligned over the center, the first defensive man to the outside of the center is numbered one. Then the defensive linemen and linebackers are numbered one, two, three, four as they appear from the inside out (Diagram 2-13).

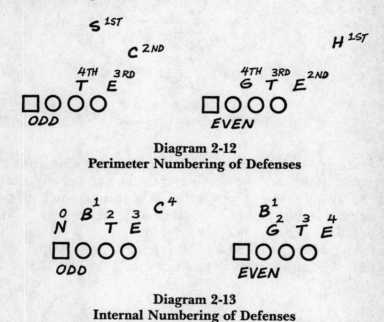

Diagram 2-12
**Perimeter Numbering of Defenses**

Diagram 2-13
**Internal Numbering of Defenses**

## BLOCKING SYSTEM

Several blocking patterns are needed to cope with all defensive alignments and stunts. Base blocking is used most often. This is the one-on-one block firing out on the closest defensive man on the side the ball is to be run. After contact, the offensive men drive their man away from the point of attack. This will create the running lane for the back to run in (Diagram 2-14).

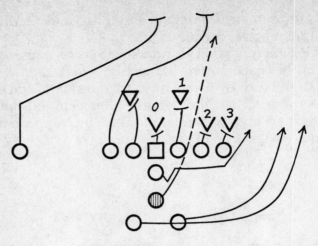

**Diagram 2-14**
**Two-Hole Base Blocking**

Wedge blocking is used in short yardage situations and against some stunts. The number of the linemen at the point of attack forms the apex of the wedge. The linemen on both sides of the man at the point of attack slide-step in and get shoulder-to-shoulder. They all block any defensive man who is in their area. The wedge blocking scheme is good against stunts, on the goal line and in short yardage situations (Diagram 2-15).

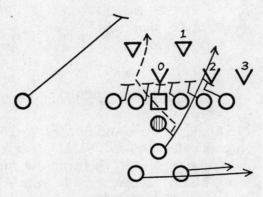

**Diagram 2-15**
**Zero-Hole Wedge Blocking**

Combination blocking is used to get desired blocking angles at the point of attack. Combination blocking uses the offensive player numbering system to get the number calls to identify each block. The linemen and backs, with the exception of the quarterback, are each given a number. The linemen have the same numbers as in the regular offensive hole numbering system. The fullback is numbered one, the left halfback numbered nine and the right halfback numbered eight (Diagram 2-16).

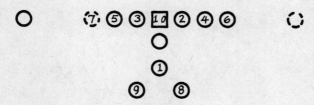

**Diagram 2-16**
**Combination Blocking Numbers**

A two- or three-digit number is called for the combination block. The number or numbers of the man or men called will block in the area of the last number called. The men outside of the last number called will block inside. Linemen are drilled to

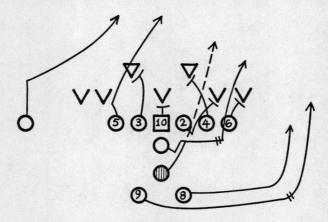

**Diagram 2-17**
**Twenty-Four (24) Block**

make calls or change them at the line of scrimmage. The calls may also be made in the huddle and changed at the line of scrimmage if the need arises. Dummy calls should be made on the side away from the point of attack to keep the defense from knowing where the ball is going to be run. Diagrams 2-17 through 2-27 show the most common combination blocks that are used.

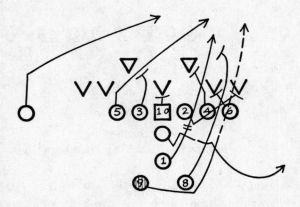

**Diagram 2-18**
**Twenty-Six (26) Block**

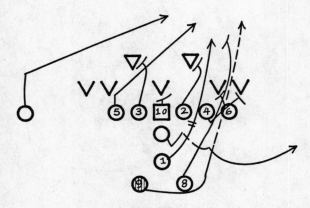

**Diagram 2-19**
**Forty-Six (46) Block**

*H*

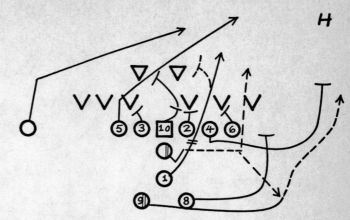

**Diagram 2-20**
**Forty-Eight (48) Block**

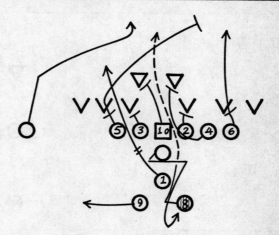

**Diagram 2-21**
**Forty-Two (42) Block**

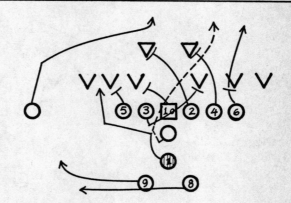

**Diagram 2-22**
**Thirty-Two (32) Block**

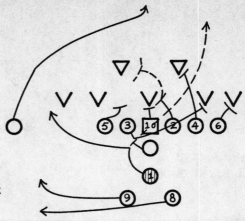

**Diagram 2-23**
**Thirty-Four (34) Block**

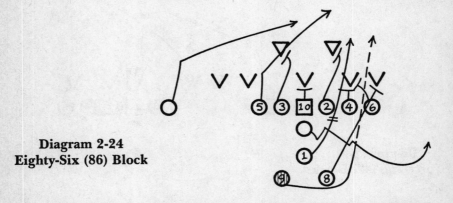

**Diagram 2-24**
**Eighty-Six (86) Block**

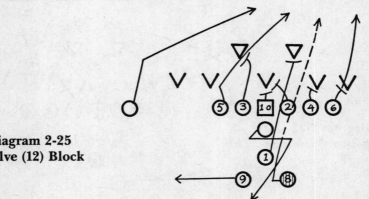

**Diagram 2-25**
**Twelve (12) Block**

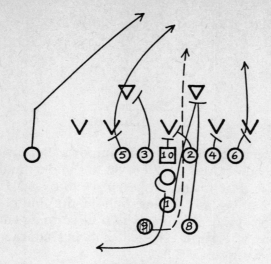

**Diagram 2-26**
**One-Eighty-Two (182) Block**

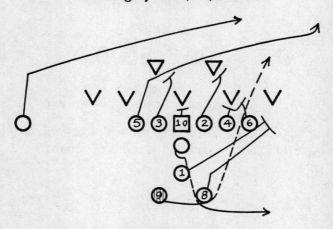

**Diagram 2-27**
**One-Eighty-Six (186) Block**

The Come-Around block is a simple variation used mostly against split-six or split-four teams. The tackle blocks in on the defensive man on the line of scrimmage. The guard pulls around the tackle to block the linebacker. This blocking adjustment allows better blocking angles on the defense for outside plays (Diagram 2-28).

**Diagram 2-28**
**Come-Around Block**

Downfield blocking is very important. It is a neglected phase of football. Many players do not understand how to get downfield and be in the proper place to block. Two rules are needed. First, release shallow behind the line of scrimmage. Second, block in the running lane. The running lane is the hole on the line of scrimmage that is being attacked, extended downfield (Diagram 2-29).

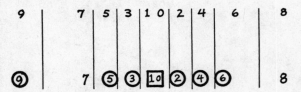

**Diagram 2-29**
**Running Lanes Extended Downfield**

Giving proper attention to details in organizing the Wishbone base will pay dividends on the scoreboard.

# CHAPTER *3*

# *Coaching the Wishbone*
# *Running Attack*

Seven running plays are used in the basic Wishbone running attack. These seven basic plays attack every hole along the line of scrimmage. The seven basic plays are the Veer, Belly, Option and Triple Option to the flow side and the Sneak,

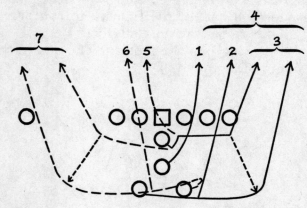

5. Sneak
6. Counter Dive
7. Counter Option

1. Veer
2. Belly
3. Option
4. Triple Option

**Diagram 3-1**
**Basic Running Plays**

Counter Dive and Counter Option to the counter flow side. The flow side offense are the plays that are run to the side of the original fake and the counter flow offense are the plays that are run away from the original fake. Each play looks alike but hits a different area of the defense (Diagram 3-1).

## VEER

The Veer is the predetermined handoff to the fullback. The left end releases downfield and blocks in the running lane with a side body block. The left tackle releases inside of the defensive man aligned on him and blocks in the running lane downfield. The left guard, center and right guard base block to the left. The right tackle base blocks to the right. The right end turns out, bumps the defensive man outside and releases downfield to block. The fullback runs a path over the outside foot of the right guard. The fullback makes a pocket, receives the ball and cuts upfield after clearing the line of scrimmage. The left halfback fakes an option play to the right. The right halfback sprints to the right on an option play course. The quarterback takes a 45-degree step with his right foot and swings the football out for the fullback to run over it while stepping to the right with his left foot. He rides with the fullback while giving him the football. The quarterback then fakes an option (Diagram 3-2).

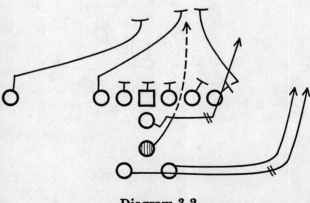

**Diagram 3-2**
**Veer**

Several blocking variations are used with the Veer play. Twenty-four blocking, with the right guard and the right tackle crossing on their blocks is good to get good blocking angles. The right tackle blocks inside first, with the right guard pulling behind him blocking outside. Everyone else blocks the same as on the Veer play with base blocking (Diagram 3-3).

The Veer may be run with Triple Option blocking. This blocking will leave the defensive tackle unblocked. A good split by the right tackle is necessary to widen the defensive tackle. All other offensive assignments remain the same (Diagram 3-4).

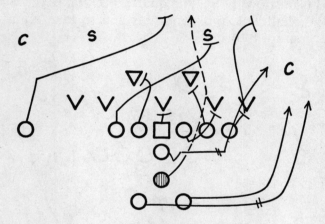

**Diagram 3-3**
**Veer With Twenty-Four Blocking**

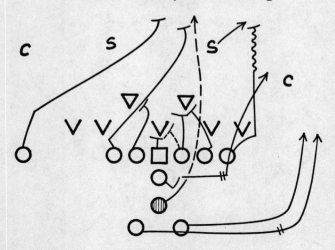

**Diagram 3-4**
**Veer with Triple Option Blocking**

The right halfback may be used to block the defensive tackle with an Eighty-four block. The right halfback must really sprint hard to get ahead of the fullback. The block really becomes a shielding type of block so the fullback can break by the defensive tackle (Diagram 3-5).

Several fakes by the other backs may be used with the Veer play. The Option fake is used most often. The Belly play is faked quite often. All assignments remain the same, except the left halfback fakes in over the outside foot of the right tackle. The right halfback drives through the right tackle, right end gap and fakes downfield. The quarterback fakes the Belly play to the left halfback and continues a pass fake after getting depth (Diagram 3-6).

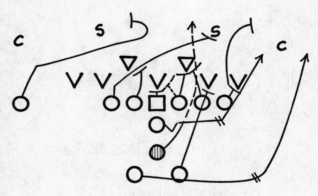

**Diagram 3-5**
**Veer with Eighty-Four Blocking**

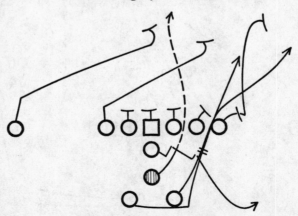

**Diagram 3-6**
**Veer with Belly Fake**

The Veer may also be executed with a Counter Dive fake. Linemen execute the regular blocks with the backs faking a Counter Dive. The left halfback takes a jab step to the right and fakes over the left guard. The right halfback jab-steps to the right and runs a Counter Option course to the left. The quarterback hands off to the fullback and then pivots to the left to fake a Counter Dive to the left halfback and continues to the left faking the Counter option to the right halfback (Diagram 3-7).

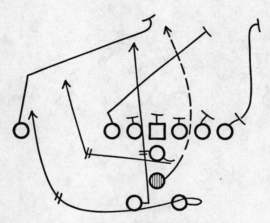

**Diagram 3-7**
**Veer with Counter Option Fake**

## BELLY

The Belly play fits into the basic Wishbone series and is an excellent play. The left end releases downfield to block in the running lane with a side body block. The left tackle bumps the defensive man over him and releases downfield to block in the running lane. The left guard, center and right guard base block the defensive men over them to the left. The right tackle blocks the defensive man over him to the inside. The right end blocks inside against the odd defense and blocks outside against the split or even defense. The fullback fakes the Veer play trying to fake so hard that he gets tackled. If the fullback does not get tackled he becomes a blocker.

The right halfback blocks out with an Eighty-Six block against the odd defense and with an Eighty-Four block on the defensive tackle against the split or even defense. The right halfback uses a shoulder block, getting his head on the left side of the defensive man. He will drive the defensive man out with a lot of leg drive. If the right halfback feels the defensive man slipping off of the shoulder block, then he drops to a scramble or crab block.

The left halfback sprints to the right and cuts upfield taking a path over the outside foot of the right tackle. The quarterback steps out, fakes the Veer to the fullback and

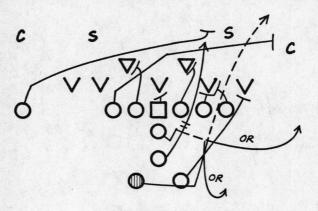

**Diagram 3-8**
**Belly Against the Odd Defense**

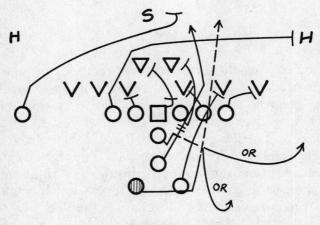

**Diagram 3-9**
**Belly Againt the Even Defense**

continues to the right to place the ball into the left halfback's pocket. The quarterback will be coming back away from the line of scrimmage after faking the Veer to the fullback and will make the handoff to the left halfback about two steps from the line of scrimmage. Then the quarterback will continue his fake by either faking a pass or a keep wide to the right (Diagrams 3-8 and 3-9).

A good blocking variation is to use combination blocking, with the right guard pulling to block out with Twenty-Six blocking against the odd defense and Twenty-Four blocking against the split or even defense. A general rule for the right guard to follow on this play with combination blocking is to block the first defensive man to show outside the right tackle (Diagrams 3-10 and 3-11).

## OPTION

The Option is different from the Triple Option in that only the defensive end is optioned instead of the defensive tackle and end in the triple option. The left end releases downfield to block. He attempts to get to the running lane but

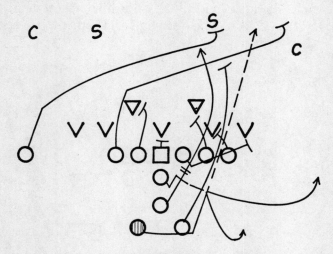

**Diagram 3-10**
**Belly Against the Odd Defense with Twenty-Six Blocking**

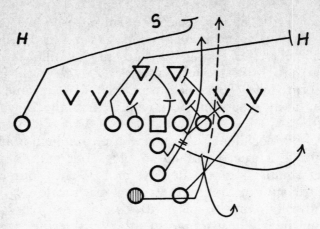

**Diagram 3-11**
**Belly Against the Even Defense with Twenty-Four Blocking**

may not be able to because of the distance involved. He will use a side body block when he does throw his block. The left tackle releases inside his defensive man and sprints downfield to block in the running lane with a side body block. All the internal linemen base block, taking their man to the left. The right end also blocks to the inside. The fullback fakes the Veer and tries to get tackled by making a very good fake. If the fullback does not get tackled, he should block on a linebacker or on downfield (Diagram 3-12). The left halfback sprints to the right

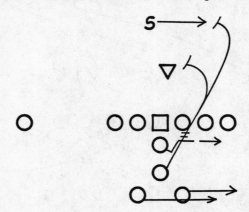

**Diagram 3-12**
**Fullback's Blocking Path for the Option**

riding the hip of the right halfback and looks for the pitch from the quarterback. If the left halfback receives the pitch, he looks to cut off the right halfback's block. The left halfback keeps a four-yard depth gap from the quarterback and should be to the quarterback's outside on the pitch (Diagram 3-13).

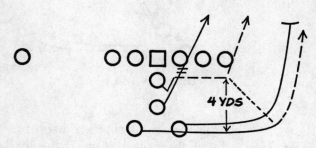

**Diagram 3-13**
**Left Halfback-Quarterback Relation on the Option**

The left halfback keeps this relationship on downfield so that he can receive a pitch at any time from the quarterback. The right halfback sprints to the right until he is three yards beyond where the tight end aligns. Then he turns upfield to block on the cornerback or halfback. As he approaches the block, he must come under control getting close to the defensive man before throwing the block. He should try to get his head close to the defensive man's chest and then turn either way, bringing his hip in contact with the defensive man's midsection, driving very hard into him.

The quarterback steps out as on a Veer, faking to the fullback. He takes a short ride-step toward the line on the fake. The quarterback's eyes pick up the defensive end and should be focused on him until the pitch or keep occurs. After the ride-step, the quarterback pushes off his left foot and sprints toward the defensive end. He makes the appropriate play according to the defensive end's actions. If the defensive end plays him, he pitches to the left halfback. If the defensive end floats or plays the pitch, the quarterback keeps inside the defensive end and cuts upfield (Diagram 3-14).

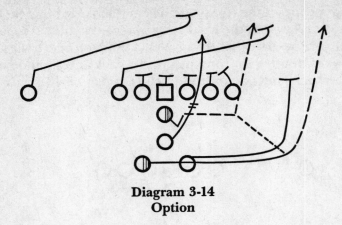

**Diagram 3-14**
**Option**

There are blocking variations that are useful to get maximum effectiveness from the option. One is the load block by the fullback. He blocks the defensive tackle after his fake and frees the right tackle to block in on the linebacker, and the right end to block downfield as he does on the triple option (Diagram 3-15).

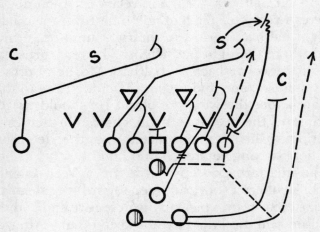

**Diagram 3-15**
**Option with Load Block by the Fullback**

There may be a load block by the right halfback on the defensive tackle, with the right end releasing outside to block on the corner. This blocking variation helps to keep the hard-crashing defensive end off the quarterback longer. The right end slows the defensive end's charge as he turns out into his path and engages him on his release to block on the corner (Diagram 3-16).

If the defensive end plays very tight on the offensive end, the defensive end may be hooked by the offensive end. All other assignments remain the same, except the quarterback will

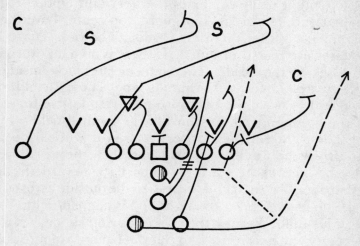

**Diagram 3-16**
**Option with Load Block by the Right Halfback**

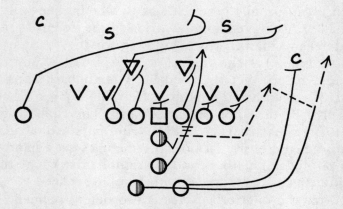

**Diagram 3-17**
**Option with Hook Block by the Right End**

now option on the first man to approach him downfield (Diagram 3-17).

## TRIPLE OPTION

This is the play that made the Wishbone famous. Proper execution makes the Triple Option impossible to stop. The Triple Option really combines the Veer and Option together. The left end, left tackle, left guard and center have the same assignments as they do in the Option. The right guard blocks the defensive man over him or, if there is no man over him, he will block to the inside. The right tackle blocks inside. This block creates the fullback's running lane. The right end releases downfield to block the defensive man responsible for defending the outside, deep one-third of the football field.

The right end first drives his man downfield deeper by releasing as he would for a pass and then throws a side body block on him as he starts to come back toward the line of scrimmage. The right end releases to the outside across the face of the defensive end if the right end is aligned tight.

The fullback runs the Veer course. He makes a good pocket for the quarterback to put the ball in. He must be alert to close the pocket on the ball if the quarterback leaves the football with him. He must not grab onto the football if the quarterback is pulling the football out of the pocket. The fullback can usually get a clue as to whether he will get the football or not by reading the action of the defensive tackle or the defensive man that is being read for the first part of the Triple Option. If the defensive man is not closing on the fullback, he will get the football. The fullback runs a Veer course if he receives the football. He will become a faker and a blocker if he does not get the football. The fullback must be able to break a partial tackle if he is running the football. This is because the defensive tackle can sometimes get a hand or arm on him. The left halfback and the right halfback have the same assignments as they carry out in the option play.

Now the quarterback reads two defensive men. He will first read the first defensive man outside the right tackle. If this man does not close down to take the fullback, the quarterback leaves the football with the fullback. If the defensive man closes, the quarterback pulls the football from the fullback's pocket and sprints toward the defensive end. The quarterback should grasp the football hard and pivot his wrists to withdraw the football. He should waggle the football when he is pulling it from the fullback. This pushes the fullback's arm out and hits his body with pressure to alert the fullback that the football will be pulled. As the quarterback approaches the defensive end, he makes the same pitch-or-keep decision as he does on the regular option play (Diagram 3-18).

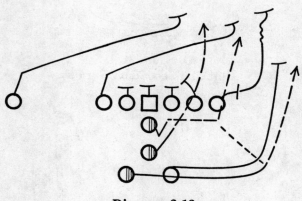

**Diagram 3-18**
**Triple Option**

The Triple Option is an excellent play to run to the split end side of the formation. In fact, it may be more effective to the split end side against some defenses that play soft to the split end side, or defenses that might overshift toward the tight end.

The right end and the right halfback must be able to recognize and block against secondary stunts. They have time to see the stunts developing as they start their routes to block. Diagrams 3-19 and 3-20 show two common stunts and the blocking adjustments.

There are some blocking variations that can help the triple option execution. One is for the right tackle and right end to change blocking assignments with a Forty-Eight block. This is a good variation to use if the linebacker flows too fast for the right tackle to block effectively (Diagram 3-21).

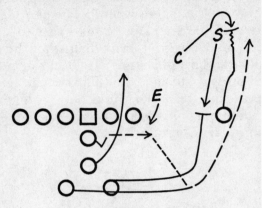

**Diagram 3-19**
**Blocking Secondary Stunts**

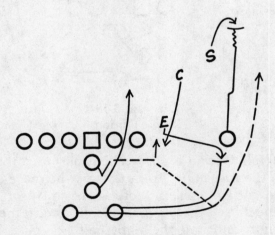

**Diagram 3-20**
**Blocking Secondary Stunts**

Counter flow plays are very important in the Wishbone offense. There is so much pressure put on the defense to try to stop the flow offense that the counter flow offense will break for long gainers.

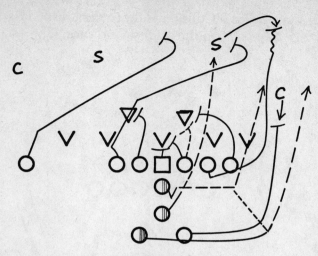

**Diagram 3-21**
**Triple Option with Forty-Eight Block**

## QUARTERBACK COUNTER

Wishbone quarterbacks should have running ability and the Quarterback Counter is a good play to take advantage of this. The play is good in normal running situations as well as for short yardage and on the goal line.

Both ends release downfield to block in the running lane. The internal linemen fire out on base blocks. The left tackle and left guard drive their men to the left. The center, right guard and right tackle drive their men to the right. The fullback fakes the Veer. The right halfback and left halfback both fake to the right as they do on the option play. The quarterback steps out to the right and fakes the Veer to the fullback before pivoting to the left and driving for the center's left foot, looking to cut upfield (Diagram 3-22).

Combination blocking variations are very effective with the Quarterback Counter. The left tackle and left guard are used to execute Thirty-Five and Fifty-Three combination blocks (Diagrams 3-23 through Diagram 3-25).

The Quarterback Counter is more than just a quarterback sneak. It is a basic play in the offense and should be used in this way.

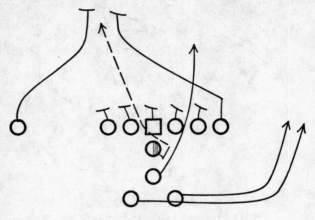

**Diagram 3-22**
**Quarterback Counter**

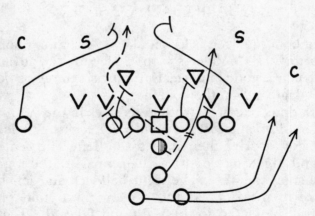

**Diagram 3-23**
**Quarterback Counter with Thirty-Five Blocking**

## COUNTER DIVE

The Counter Dive is the most explosive play in the Wishbone besides the Triple Option. This is because the play develops very quickly and also has good misdirection.

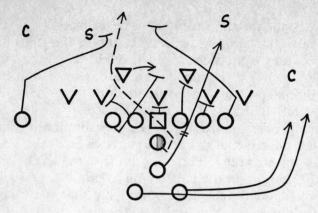

**Diagram 3-24**
**Quarterback Counter with Fifty-Three Blocking**
**Against an Odd Defense**

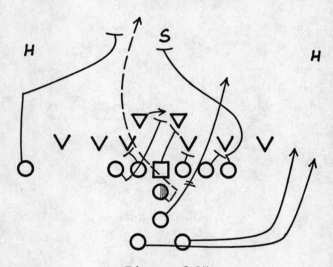

**Diagram 3-25**
**Quarterback Counter with Fifty-Three Blocking**
**Against an Even Defense**

The left end releases downfield to block with a side body block in the running lane. The left tackle base blocks out to the left. The left guard will base block his man either way that he can take him. The center, right guard and right tackle all base block to the right. The right end releases downfield to side body block in the running lane. The fullback fakes the Veer play. The right halfback takes a jab step to the right and then runs a counter option course to the left. The counter option course is just like a regular option path, except that there is a jab counter-step to the opposite direction.

The left halfback takes a jab step to the right and then drives for the left guard's hips, receives the handoff and runs off the left guard's block. The quarterback fakes the Veer to the fullback, pivots to the left and hands off to the left halfback. He then continues on to the left, faking a counter option. The left halfback should hit the hole so quickly that the quarterback must hustle to reach him and hand him the football (Diagram 3-26).

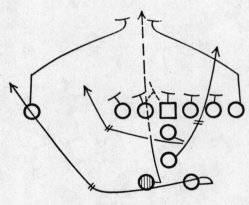

**Diagram 3-26**
**Counter Dive**

Combination blocking is used with the Counter Dive. Thirty-Five, Fifty-Three and Thirteen blocking is used (Diagrams 3-27 through 3-31).

There are two different faking actions in the backfield that can be useful against some defenses. Fast pursuing linebackers who move quickly with the initial flow of the backfield can be hurt with the fake of the right halfback going to the right as he does on the option instead of faking to the left. If this action is used in the backfield, the quarterback will drop and fake a pass after handing off the the left halfback (Diagram 3-32).

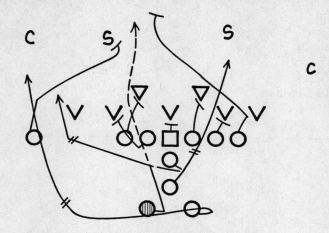

Diagram 3-27
Counter Dive with Thirty-Five Blocking Against an
Odd Defense

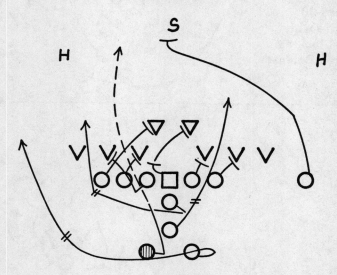

Diagram 3-28
Counter Dive with Thirty-Five Blocking Against an Even Defense

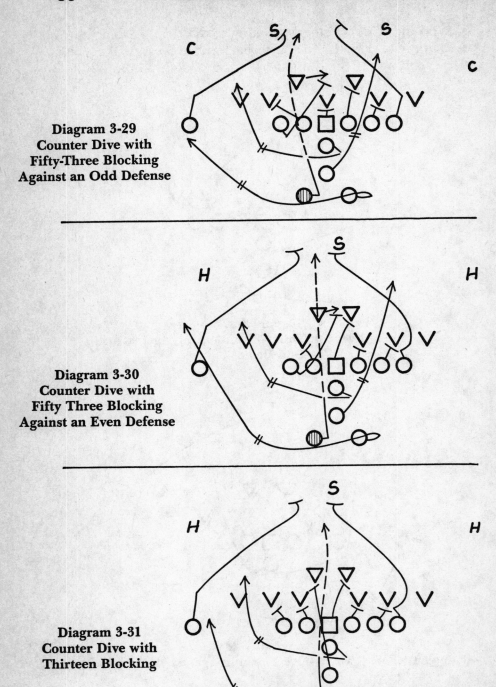

**Diagram 3-29
Counter Dive with
Fifty-Three Blocking
Against an Odd Defense**

**Diagram 3-30
Counter Dive with
Fifty Three Blocking
Against an Even Defense**

**Diagram 3-31
Counter Dive with
Thirteen Blocking**

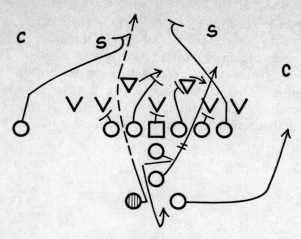

**Diagram 3-32**
**Counter Dive with Right Halfback Faking to the Right**

If the Counter Option is being very successful, the use of the Counter Option fake with the fullback can help the Counter Dive play. The fullback takes a jab step to the right, pivots and sprints to the left and cuts upfield to block in the nine-hole area. He cuts just behind the diving left halfback (Diagram 3-33).

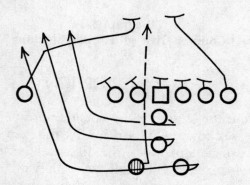

**Diagram 3-33**
**Counter Dive with the Fullback Faking the Counter Option**

One other Counter Dive blocking variation is used against split-six or split-four defenses. The blocking is called "Split Blocking." It only affects the left guard, center and right guard in their blocking assignments. Scouting reports and film study must determine if the onside defensive linebacker will flow enough to the veer fake so that he will not have to be blocked. Both guards block out on the defensive guards. The center blocks the offside linebacker. All other players have the same assignments. The right halfback will fake to the right to influence the onside linebacker. The left halfback will look to cut off the center's block after receiving the handoff (Diagram 3-34).

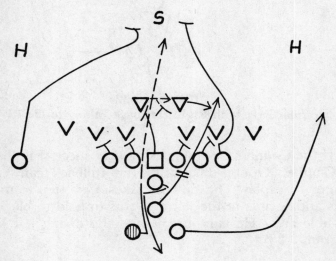

**Diagram 3-34**
**Counter Dive with "Split Blocking"**

## COUNTER OPTION

The Counter Option is the outside misdirection play. The left end releases downfield hard for five to seven steps. Then he turns to the inside to block the first defensive pursuit that comes across the field. The left tackle, left guard, center and right guard all base block taking their defensive men to the right. The right tackle fires out into the man aligned on him for one count and then releases downfield to block in the running lane. The right end also releases downfield and blocks in the running lane. The fullback takes a jab step to the right and then goes quickly to the left to block the contain man. He must time his cut to the left to clear just behind the diving left halfback.

The left halfback fakes the Counter Dive play very hard. He tries to get tackled on his fake. The right halfback takes a jab step to the right and then goes on an option path to the left, looking for the pitch from the quarterback. The quarterback takes a jab step to the right as he does on the Counter Dive except that there is no fullback to fake to. Then he pivots to the left and fakes the Counter Dive to the left halfback. After the fake, he continues down the line of scrimmage focusing all his attention on the defensive end whom he options. If the defensive end closes on him, he pitches to the trailing right halfback. If the defensive end floats or contains to the outside, the quarterback keeps and cuts upfield (Diagram 3-35).

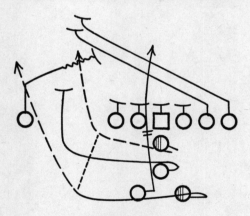

**Diagram 3-35**
**Counter Option**

One variation is used with the Counter Option. The variation should be run to the tight end side for blocking purposes. Three players are involved in the variation. The left end blocks to the inside. The left tackle pulls and executes a Fifty-Nine block. The fullback fakes the Veer play. This variation has two backs faking to the inside and yet the ball is going to be run to the outside (Diagram 3-36).

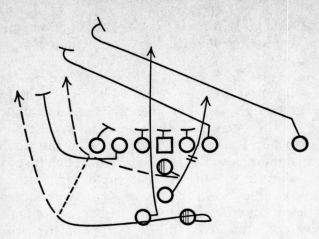

**Diagram 3-36**
**Counter Option Variation**

# CHAPTER *4*

# *Coaching the Wishbone*
# *Passing Attack*

The Wishbone is not famous as a passing formation. The passing game has never reached its potential because the running game has been so successful that Wishbone teams have not had to pass. The running success of the Wishbone makes the passing game more effective. Defenses have to be so concerned about the running game that receivers will be open and the passer will have more time to pass.

The play action pass blends in with the running attack to put maximum pressure on all the defense. In this way the pass and run complement each other.

## PASSING TREE

A passing tree naming pass routes is necessary in developing the passing attack. Diagram 4-1 shows the passing tree for the basic passing attack.

A passing chart giving the responsibility of the backs and ends is shown in Diagram 4-2.

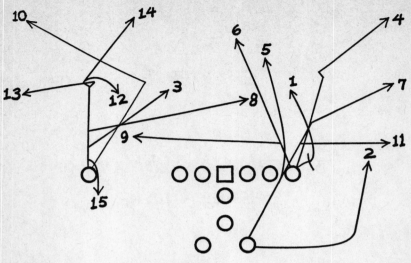

| 1. Hot | 6. Streak | 11. Flat |
|---|---|---|
| 2. Flare | 7. Out | 12. Curl |
| 3. Slant | 8. Cross | 13. Sideline |
| 4. Flag | 9. Drag | 14. Post |
| 5. Bend | 10. In and Out | 15. Quick Screen |

**Diagram 4-1**
**Passing Tree**

| Pass | Onside End | Offside End | Onside Halfback | Offside Halfback | Fullback |
|---|---|---|---|---|---|
| Hot | Hot | Slant | Flare | Block | Fake |
| Cross | Streak | Cross | Out | Block | Fake |
| Divide | Flag | Flag | Bend | Block | Fake |
| Bootleg | In & Out | Drag | Flare | Block | Fake |
| Veer | Flag | Drag | Flat | Block | Fake |

**Diagram 4-2**
**Passing Chart**

# PASS PROTECTION

The type of pass protection that is used is important. The pass protection should first make the defense think that a running play is being executed. It must also give the quarterback time to make his throw. The aggressive fire-out block, as in a running play, and keeping contact with the defensive man is good for the Wishbone play action passes. All covered linemen execute the aggressive fire-out block. The uncovered linemen will start a fire-out block and then pull up to look for a stunt or blitz. The uncovered left guard or center will drop to block on the back side (Diagrams 4-3 and 4-4).

**Diagram 4-3
Pass Protection**

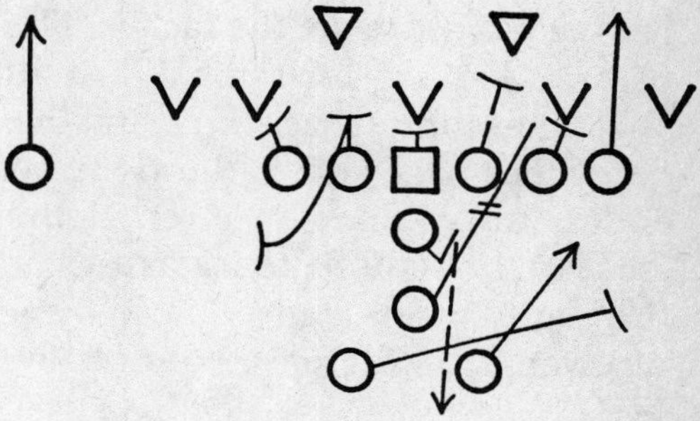

**Diagram 4-4
Pass Protection**

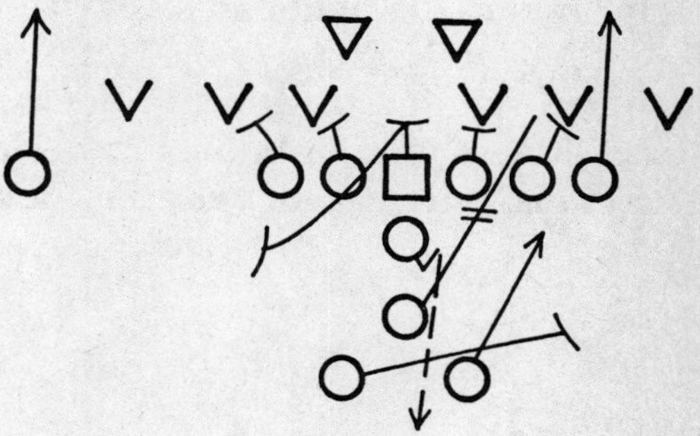

Passes are selected to hit every area of the defensive secondary and to take advantage of secondary stunts or weakness. Yet all the pass routes are simple to execute.

## HOT PASS

The Hot Pass is usually executed to take advantage of linebackers who blitz or do not drop to cover the hook area. The left end runs a slant route. He will try to block in the safety area if he does not get the pass thrown to him. All internal linemen block out aggressively with the uncovered left guard or center dropping back to block on the back side. The right end releases to the outside and goes upfield looking for the pass. He adjusts his route to get away from the linebacker on his side.

The fullback fakes the Veer play very hard. The fullback's fake must freeze the linebackers. The left halfback sprints to the right, pulling up to block just outside the right tackle. If the ball is passed to the right halfback and is intercepted, the left halfback must make the tackle. The right halfback runs a flare pattern, looking for the ball just after turning upfield.

The quarterback fakes to the fullback on the Veer and then steps back and to the right to deliver the ball to the right end as his primary receiver. If the right end is not open, he looks to the right halfback as a second choice. He then looks for the slanting left end. The left end can become the primary receiver if the defense continually leaves him open (Diagram 4-5).

The Hot Pass may be thrown to the split end. He will run a slant pattern and everyone else will execute as they do on the Hot Pass to the tight end side (Diagram 4-6).

A good variation of the Hot Pass can be combined with the Option running play. All the linemen block as they do on the regular Option, except the left tackle who blocks on the line of scrimmage instead of releasing downfield. This is because a

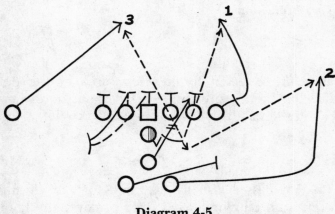

**Diagram 4-5**
**Hot Pass**

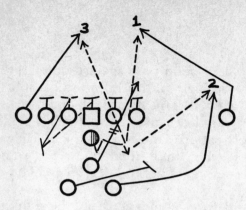

**Diagram 4-6**
**Hot Pass Variation**

forward pass may be thrown and he would be an ineligible downfield receiver. The right end will still release and run a Hot route. The fullback still fakes the Veer. The halfbacks execute as they do on the regular option. The quarterback fakes the Veer to the fullback and continues on down the line, looking for the right end on his Hot route. If the right end is open, the quarterback hits him with the pass. If the right end is covered, the quarterback continues on down the line and options the defensive end with a pitch or keep just as he does on the regular option play (Diagram 4-7).

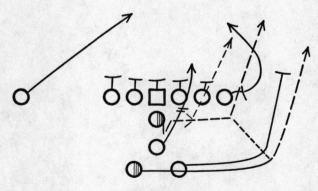

**Diagram 4-7**
**Hot Pass and Option Variation**

## CROSS PASS

   This is a very good pass against either a three- or four-deep defense. The left end will shorten his split three or four yards if he is opened. This is to allow him to cross the defense enough to get into the open area created by the other receivers. He runs a cross pattern 11 to 14 yards deep. He will cut in front of the right end who runs a streak route. The right end will run through the safety to take the safety deep. The fullback fakes the Veer.

   The left halfback comes across to the right and blocks the defensive end. He sets up just outside the offensive right tackle. The right halfback runs an out pattern about eight yards deep. The quarterback fakes the Veer to the fullback and then drops quickly to seven yards depth and steps up to throw. He looks for the left end first, the right halfback, second and the right end, third (Diagrams 4-8 and 4-9).

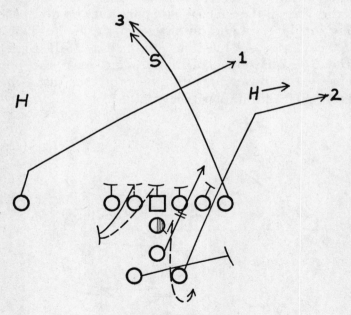

**Diagram 4-8**
**Cross Pass Against Three-Deep Defense**

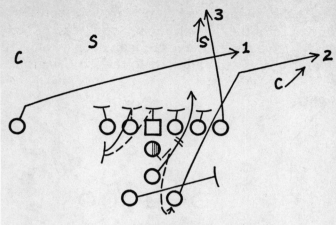

**Diagram 4-9**
**Cross Pass Against Four-Deep Defense**

## DIVIDE PASS

The Divide Pass is good against four-deep corner defenses. The offensive ends should have good splits. They both release with speed and go wide on their release. They run right at the safeties to make them cover the ends. The internal linemen carry out their regular pass protection. The fullback fakes the Veer very hard. The left halfback comes across and blocks on the defensive end. He sets up to block just outside of the offensive tackle. The right halfback releases on a bend pattern. He finds daylight just outside the right tackle to release on downfield. He looks for the ball over his left shoulder. The offensive ends and right halfback try to get a three-on-two situation deep against the defensive safeties. The quarterback uses the same mechanics as on the divide pattern and looks for the right halfback first, or the end on the side that a defensive safety comes in to cover the right halfback (Diagram 4-10).

## VEER BOOTLEG PASS

Faking the run in one direction and passing in the opposite direction is done with the Veer Bootleg Pass. The left end releases downfield as if he is going to block to the right. He then reads the defensive secondary man responsible for the deep one-third of the field on the left end's side. When the left end sees he can beat this defensive man deep outside, he pivots quickly and sprints out and deep to the left (Diagram 4-11).

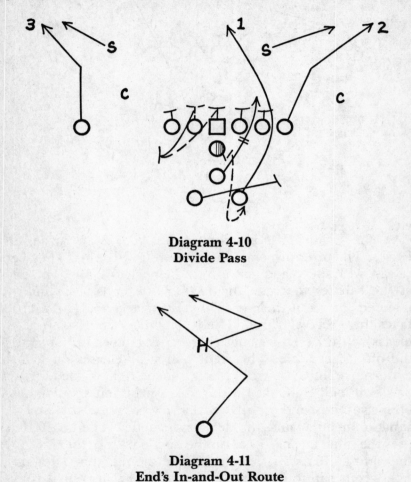

**Diagram 4-10**
**Divide Pass**

**Diagram 4-11**
**End's In-and-Out Route**

The left tackle must reach-block out on the defensive tackle. The left guard blocks the man over him. The center blocks the man over him or to the back side. The right guard pulls to the left, looking to block the defensive end either in or out. He will prefer to block him in. The right tackle check-blocks in the area where the right guard pulled from. The right end releases with a drag route seven to nine yards deep.

The fullback fakes a Veer. If he is not tackled, he continues to run an out pattern. The left halfback starts an option route to the right and then pulls up and blocks. The right halfback runs a bend route down the middle. The quarterback fakes the Veer play to the fullback and then sprints to the left hiding the ball on his hip. The quarterback must read the right guard's block and adjust his course accordingly. If the right guard hooks the defensive end in, the quarterback sprints to the outside. If the right guard kicks out on the defensive end, the quarterback pulls up short to throw (Diagrams 4-12 and 4-13).

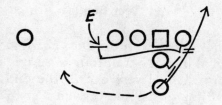

**Diagram 4-12**
**Right Guard, Quarterback Coordination on Veer Bootleg**

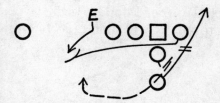

**Diagram 4-13**
**Right Guard, Quarterback Coordination on Veer Bootleg**

After reading the right guard's block and adjusting his course, the quarterback looks downfield to read the secondary and receivers. He looks for the left end first, the right end, second, and the right halfback, third. Some defenses may leave the right haflback or the fullback open. If this happens, these receivers should tell the quarterback and he can look for them first when the Veer Bootleg is run again. Diagram 4-14 shows the total Veer Bootleg.

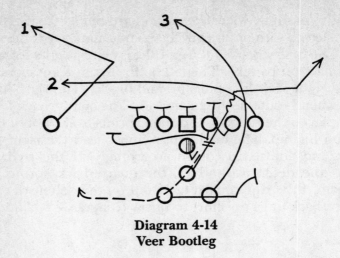

**Diagram 4-14**
**Veer Bootleg**

The Veer Bootleg, with the ends changing assignments, is good on the goal line or when four to seven yards are needed for a first down. All players except the ends have the same assignment as they do on the regular Veer Bootleg. The left end now runs a quick out route and he must look for the ball to be thrown quickly. The right end will now run a deep cross route. The quarterback must be prepared to throw quicker than on the regular Veer Bootleg. If the left end is not open on the quick out route, he will turn quickly and sprint downfield

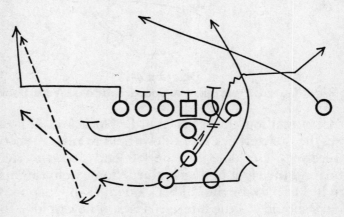

**Diagram 4-15**
**Veer Bootleg Quick**

on a streak route. The quarterback will pump-fake, drop and look for the left end long. This can be an automatic or predetermined part of the Veer Bootleg Quick (Diagram 4-15).

A good Veer Bootleg variation is to get three receivers to one side so the quarterback can see all three easily. Also the blocking scheme does not have the guard pulling. All line assignments remain the same as on the regular Veer Bootleg except the right guard and right tackle block the men aligned on them. The fullback and the quarterback also execute the same as on the regular Veer Bootleg. The left halfback jab-steps to the right and then runs a flat route to the left. The right halfback jab-steps to the right and then goes to the left to block the defensive end (Diagram 4-16).

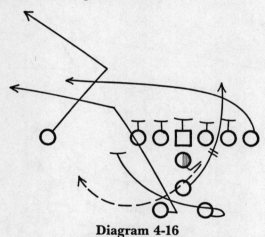

**Diagram 4-16**
**Veer Bootleg Variation**

## VEER KEEP PASS

The Veer Keep Pass has a Veer fake and a pass to the side of the fake. The left end runs a drag route seven to nine yards deep. The internal linemen all carry out the regular pass blocking with all the linemen firing out aggressively on their blocks and keeping contact with their man. The uncovered left guard or center drops back to block on the back side. The right end fakes a block to the inside and then releases on a flag route. The fullback fakes a Veer play.

The left halfback comes to the right on an option route and blocks the defensive end in. He only blocks out on the defensive end if the defensive end boxes to contain. The right halfback releases on a flat route five to seven yards deep. The quarterback fakes a Veer to the fullback and then gets depth and width, sprinting to the right. He looks for the right end first, the right halfback, second and the left end, third. The quarterback has a good running opportunity if no receiver is open. He should call "Block" and run (Diagram 4-17).

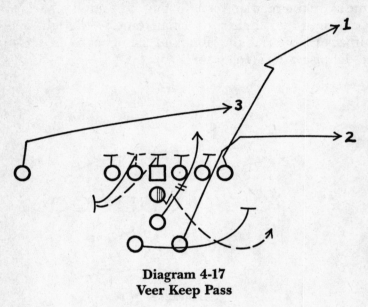

**Diagram 4-17**
**Veer Keep Pass**

## QUICK SCREEN

The Quick Screen to the split end is very effective if single coverage is used by the defense and this single coverage is by the defensive halfback. The left end drives off the line of scrimmage for two or three steps, very fast. Then he steps back to about his aligned position to receive the quick pass out to him. Upon receiving the football, he looks for the running lane that is formed by the pulling linemen. The left tackle will fire out for one count and then go to the left for about four yards, pivot back to the inside and block the first opponent from the inside out. The left guard will fire out for one count and then pull to the left about three yards beyond the left tackle's pull. He will block any opponent to show from the outside. The center will also fire out for one count and then pull to the left and turn upfield between the left tackle and left guard to block downfield. If no opponent shows for either the left tackle or left guard to block, they will go on upfield to block. The right side of the line all base block aggressively. The left halfback goes quickly to the right to block. The right halfback fakes to the right. The fullback fakes the Veer. The quarterback fakes the Veer, steps back and quickly passes to the left end (Diagram 4-18).

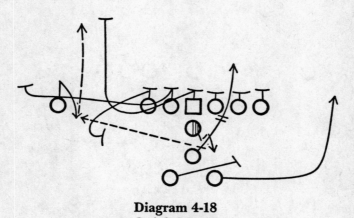

**Diagram 4-18**
**Quick Screen**

## INDIVIDUAL SPLIT END ROUTES

Individual routes are run by the split end. The split end is the best pass receiver and many defenses will try to defend him one-on-one because of the run pressure that the Wishbone has. This will enable the split end to run routes and continually be open. The individual routes that are used are the Slant, Curl, Sideline, Flag and Post. They will be called according to the defensive alignment, reactions of the defense and the coverage that is used. The Veer fake is used on all the individual routes. Regular pass protection is used on all the individual routes that are called. The individual routes can be called to or away from the Veer fake. The routes run by the other receivers will be used to further help the split end to be open or to get themselves open if the split end is covered.

The Slant pattern for the split end is called against a loose-playing defensive halfback and if there is no walk-a-way linebacker (Diagrams 4-19 and 4-20).

The Curl pattern by the split end is called against a defensive halfback who drops quickly and if there is no walk-a-

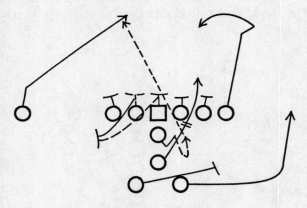

**Diagram 4-19**
**Slant Pass**

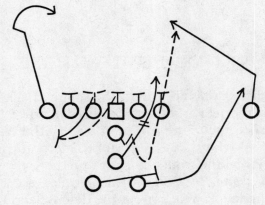

**Diagram 4-20**
**Slant Pass**

way linebacker to the split end side. The depth of the Curl can be called in the huddle (Diagrams 4-21 and 4-22).

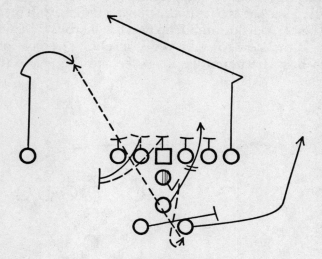

**Diagram 4-21**
**Curl Pass**

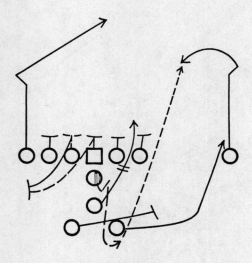

**Diagram 4-22**
**Curl Pass**

The Sideline pattern is called against the defensive half-back who is inside-conscious or who rolls quickly to the fake of a run (Diagram 4-23).

The Flag pattern is used against a defensive halfback who can be beaten outside and deep because he rolls up quickly on a fake or is too slow to cover the split end. The Post pattern is used to beat the defensive man deep to the inside (Diagram 4-24).

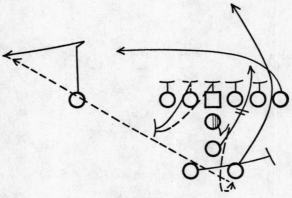

**Diagram 4-23**
**Sideline Pass**

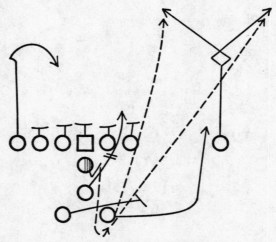

**Diagram 4-24**
**Flag and Post Passes**

# CHAPTER *5*

# *Concealing the Triple Option in the Wishbone*

The Triple Option is the most difficult play in football to defense. Any team that lines up in the Wishbone should make the defense set up to stop the triple option. This will help other offensive plays to be successful. This can be accomplished by having plays that greatly resemble the full triple option.

There may be times when you feel that your team cannot execute the full triple option. Inexperience or injury, especially in the backfield, or poor field conditions may limit the proper execution of the triple option.

1. Veer
2. Keep
3. Pitch
4. Option
5. Triple Option

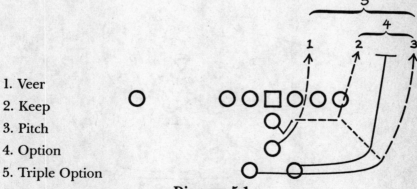

**Diagram 5-1**
**Play Pattern of the Triple Option and Predetermined Plays**

Inexperienced teams can gradually build up to executing the triple option by using plays that have segments of the triple option in it.

The play pattern of the backs in the triple option and the predetermined plays are alike. There is an element of concealing in this factor alone (Diagram 5-1).

## VEER WITH TRIPLE OPTION BLOCKING

This is the predetermined give to the fullback with the linemen carrying out triple option blocking. The important coaching point is for the right tackle—he takes a maximum split. On his charge on the snap of the ball, he flips his outside arm up and tries to make contact with the defensive tackle to his outside. He steps out with a six-inch jab step to make the contact. Then he steps back inside to block with his triple option blocking. The wider split is to get the defensive man out wider, and contact is to prevent the defensive man from slanting into the fullback's running lane. The Veer with triple option blocking is successful with either the small, quick fullback or the big, strong fullback. The small, quick fullback will run past the unblocked defensive tackle because of the right tackle's action and the fullback's quickness. The bigger, stronger fullback can execute the play successfully but will sometimes have to break an arm tackle by the defensive tackle (Diagram 5-2).

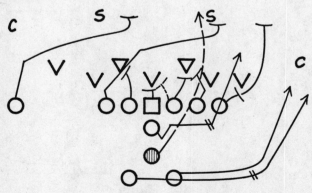

**Diagram 5-2**
**Veer with Triple Option Blocking**

## KEEP

The Keep by the quarterback is a good play for several reasons. It is a good play in the goal line offense. It is also a good short-yardage play. There is less chance of a fumble since no handoff is made. The line executes the same blocks as they do on the option play. The left end and left tackle both release to block downfield in the running lane. All the other linemen execute base blocks to the inside. The fullback and the left halfback also execute the same as they do on the option play. The right halfback blocks the defensive end out with an Eighty-Six block. This is a shoulder block with his head on the left side of the defensive man. The quarterback fakes the Veer to the fullback and continues on down the line toward the defensive end as he would on the option. He will fake a pitch to the left halfback and cut upfield in the running lane created by the block of the right end to the inside and the right halfback to the outside (Diagram 5-3).

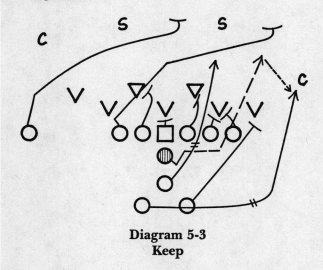

Diagram 5-3
Keep

## VEER KEEP OPTION

The Veer Keep Option combines the Veer and the Keep in one play and uses triple option blocking. This is a good play for the inexperienced, as well as the veteran, quarterback. The quarterback has only the inside read of the triple option to execute but the total play looks like the triple option to the defense. The Veer Keep Option greatly resembles the triple option for there is only one blocking change between the two plays. The right halfback will block the defensive end out after the right end bumps him on his release outside to block downfield. The quarterback will read the first defensive man aligned outside the offensive tackle. If that defensive man is not slanting inside, the quarterback leaves the football with the fullback. If this defensive man slants to the inside, the quarterback pulls the football from the fullback's pocket and executes the Keep portion of the play by cutting upfield in the running lane between the right end and right halfback's block. The quarterback has the lateral option to the trailing left halfback on downfield. The left halfback must keep a four-yard reference outside and slightly behind in order to get the lateral pitch properly.

The linemen should get maximum splits. The right end should flex to get the defensive end out wider on the Veer Keep Option (Diagram 5-4).

One variation of the Veer Keep Option is for the right end and the right halfback to change blocking assignments (Diagram 5-5).

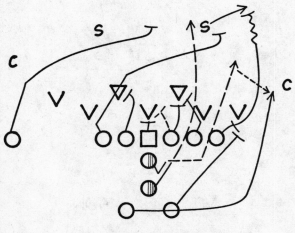

**Diagram 5-4**
**Veer Keep Option**

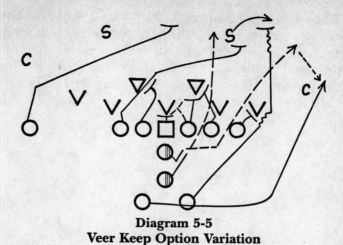

**Diagram 5-5**
**Veer Keep Option Variation**

## CORNER OPTION

The Corner Option is good to use against the crashing defensive end or the defensive end who lines up so tight that he can be hook blocked by the right halfback. All other offensive assignments are the same as on the regular option play. The quarterback will now keep on down the line and cut up field outside the right halfback's block on the defensive end. He will then option the corner or contain man of the defense. The left halfback trails to get a possible pitch (Diagram 5-6).

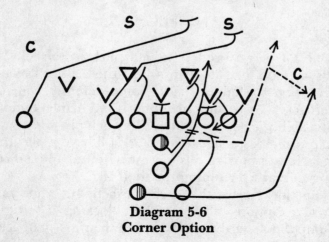

**Diagram 5-6**
**Corner Option**

The Corner Option can be run with Forty-Eight blocking by the right tackle. He should pass up the contain man of the defense because the contain man will be optioned. This means that the right tackle will block the secondary man responsible for the deep outside third of the secondary. His block will be the same as that of the right end on the triple option play (Diagram 5-7).

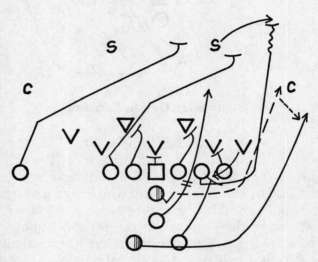

**Diagram 5-7**
**Corner Option with Forty-Eight Blocking**

## PITCH

The Pitch is a predetermined pitch to the left halfback. This is a good play to run when the halfbacks are better runners than the quarterback. Some defenses will force the quarterback to run on the option and triple option if his running ability is not very good. The pitch provides a way to get the ball to the best ball carriers and still have a play that looks like the triple option. In this way the defense cannot dictate who is going to end up running the football.

The blocking for the Pitch is exactly the same as it is for the Corner Option with Forty-Eight blocking. The right tackle will bump the defensive end to set up the right halfback's block.

He will then block the contain man to clear a running lane for the ball carrier. The quarterback fakes the Veer and comes on down the line just as he would do in the option play. He will execute a pitch to the left halfback as he comes close to the defensive end. He will then cut upfield and block on pursuit coming across toward the play (Diagram 5-8).

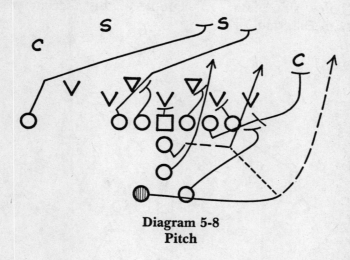

**Diagram 5-8**
**Pitch**

## VEER BELLY OPTION

The Veer Belly Option combines the Veer and the Belly plays with triple option blocking. The Veer Belly Option is executed just like the Veer Keep Option except the quarterback either hands off to the fullback or the left halfback. All other assignments remain the same (Diagram 5-9).

## VARYING THE BLOCKING ROUTE

The defense can key the onside halfback's route on blocking assignments. If the onside halfback will vary his routes, the defense will be confused about their keys. On all plays to the right, the right halfback takes one of two approaches to his blocking assignments. He either goes toward the defensive end on about a 45-degree angle or he goes directly toward the sideline at about 90 degrees for several steps before cutting upfield to block (Diagram 5-10).

The onside halfback can take a route toward the defensive end at a 45-degree angle, flatten out into the flat and turn upfield to block on all wide plays. He can use this alternate path on all flow side plays. An example of this alternate route is shown in Diagram 5-11.

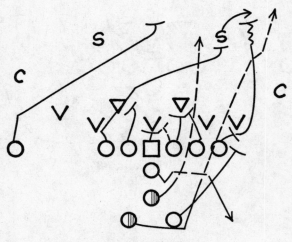

**Diagram 5-9**
**Veer Belly Option**

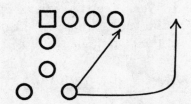

**Diagram 5-10**
**Onside Halfback's Blocking Route**

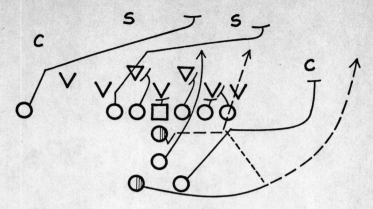

**Diagram 5-11**
**Option with Right Halfback's Alternate**
**Blocking Route**

# CHAPTER 6

# Utilizing Complementary Plays
# to the Wishbone Base

Seven running plays make up the basic Wishbone running offense. Six passes with additional individual routes make up the basic Wishbone passing attack. Game situations or opponent's tendencies picked up in scouting or film study provide opportunities to use complementary plays to an effective basic offense. Those situations and opponent tendencies are:

1. Long down and distance.
2. Type of defense used by the opposition.
3. Unusual individual defensive reaction.
4. Time remaining in the half or game.
5. Score.
6. When it is sensed that the opponent is looking for a certain play, fake it and run something else.
7. Getting the best ball carrier and best blockers against some defensive weakness.
8. The addition of three complementary plays will allow the halfbacks to hit all areas along the line of scrimmage (Diagram 6-1).

Fourteen complementary plays are discussed. All complementary plays should not be included at one time. Add them as the players learn and master them. Also, complementary plays can be added or dropped from week to week according to the opponent's style of play. The complementary plays are not basic ones and should not take up as much practice time.

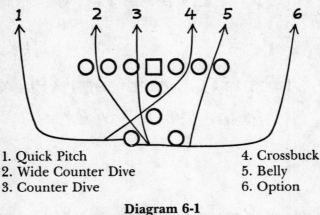

1. Quick Pitch
2. Wide Counter Dive
3. Counter Dive

4. Crossbuck
5. Belly
6. Option

**Diagram 6-1**
**Halfback's Running Areas**

## WIDE REVERSE

The Wide Reverse is valuable in that it can be used successfully against fast-flowing defenses or against a back side defensive end or tackle who is responsible for trailing containment and does not do it properly. The split end who has speed and running ability runs the wide reverse. Base blocking is used on the flow or initial fake side of the line. This means that the left tackle and left guard will fire out on base blocks. Screen blocking is used on the offside or the side away from the initial flow fake. The center, right guard and right tackle are involved in the screen blocking. They fire out aggressively for two counts. Then they slip off and carry out their individual assignments.

The three screen blockers should make it appear to their opponents that they have been beaten on their blocks. The right tackle peels out for approximately four yards and pivots back to the inside and blocks the first opponent from the inside

out. If no one shows for him to block, he should lead the play
downfield. The right guard pulls and goes beyond the right
tackle for approximately three yards to a total of eight yards
from his base alignment. He blocks the first man to show from
the outside. If no one shows, he leads the play downfield. The
center pulls and leads the play down the alley between the right
tackle and the right guard's blocking alley. This creates a
running lane for the ball carrier. The right end blocks inside
for two counts and then he releases shallow as he does on a
running play away from him. Then he sprints to get into the
running lane to block to the inside.

The fullback fakes the Veer play very hard. The left
halfback blocks the first man to show outside the left tackle's
block. The right halfback fakes an option to the left. His path is
a little deeper to allow the split end a path to run in. The
quarterback steps out to the left, fakes a veer to the fullback
and continues on down the line as he does on the option to the
left. After two steps past the Veer fake, the quarterback pitches
to the split end who has jab-stepped upfield, pivoted and run a
course just inside the right halfback's path. The pitch is timed
so it looks as if the right halfback is going to receive it, but the
split end takes it going in the opposite direction at the last
moment. Upon receiving the pitch, the split end continues full

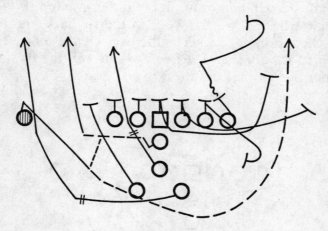

**Diagram 6-2**
**Wide Reverse**

speed to the right to get into the screen blocker's running lane. The split end may have to give some ground or get more depth to get around the right tackle's block (Diagram 6-2).

## END-AROUND

The end-around play is very good to use if the counter flow offense is a strong threat. The defense must be concerned about the counter dive and counter option plays in the basic running attack. The end-around play could be termed a counter flow counter play. The fake of the counter dive is the secret to the success of the end-around. The left end steps back one step, gains depth and receives the handoff from the quarterback. He continues on this angle until he clears the right halfback's original alignment. Then he reads the right halfback's block and runs accordingly. The left end will prefer to run outside. All the internal linemen base block to their left. The right end also base blocks to the inside. The fullback fakes the Veer and then levels off, sprinting to the right to block in the running lane. The left halfback fakes the counter dive very hard. He must freeze the internal defense. The right halfback fakes the first two counter dive steps and then sprints to the right to hook the defensive end in with a shoulder block. The right halfback will block out on the defensive end if he boxes. The quarterback fakes the Veer to the fullback, the counter dive to the left halfback, keeps the ball for one more step and hands off to the left end. After handing off, the quarterback continues the counter option fake (Diagram 6-3).

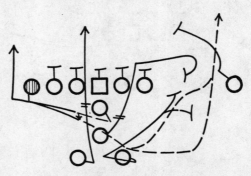

**Diagram 6-3**
**End-Around**

## BELLY KEEP OUTSIDE

The Belly Keep Outside is a companion play to the Belly play. It is a play that can break for long gains when the Belly play has been successful and the faking is carried out properly. The left end releases downfield and executes a side body block in the running lane. The left tackle also releases downfield and blocks in the running lane. All the internal linemen will base block to their left. The right end also base blocks to the inside. The fullback fakes the Veer and then levels off and sprints to the right to block in the running lane. The left halfback fakes the Belly play very hard to freeze the defense. The right halfback goes straight at the defensive end as if to block him out as he does on the Belly play. Then, at the last moment, he drives his head past the defensive end and blocks him to the inside. The quarterback fakes the Veer to the fullback, Belly to the left halfback and then keeps the ball the ball himself. He hides the ball on his hip and sprints with great speed to the outside (Diagram 6-4).

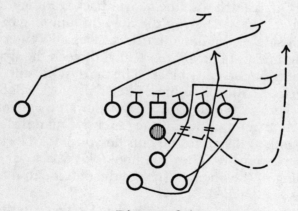

**Diagram 6-4**
**Belly Keep Outside**

## QUICK PITCH

The Quick Pitch is probably not used enough in football today. It has been used with success in all T formation offenses, and can be used with great success in the Wishbone also. It will be helpful to align the halfbacks out six to twelve inches wider on the quick pitch. This may be in keeping with the trend of some Wishbone teams that have their halfbacks align behind their guards who have splits of two to three feet.

The Quick Pitch is very good against teams that are looking for the play to come inside. It gives the halfback a play to go wide to his side of the line. This is very helpful if the halfbacks' speeds are not close to being equal and the coach wants a play to get the faster halfback wide to the faster halfback's side.

The Quick Pitch can be used two ways. One is to call it to one side and have a predetermined play. The other is to have the quarterback look over the defense and pitch to the halfback who he thinks has the greater chance of success according to the defensive alignment. The predetermined pitch would be better for the inexperienced quarterback to execute and the reading of the defense before the snap and pitching to the halfback having the best running advantage according to the defensive alignment would be better for the experienced quarterback.

The Quick Pitch with the quarterback reading the defense has the center base blocking the man on him or gap to either side. Each side of the line, guards, tackles and ends, have the same assignments. The guards pull and block the first pursuit to show outside the end's block. The tackles pull and block the cornerback or halfback to their side. This block will be a quick kick-out block if the defensive man flows up fast or a block made after turning upfield if the defensive man is slow to flow up. The ends will step to the outside and hook block the first man to their outside. They will hook block back to the inside. The pulling of the linemen freezes the defense to the side that the ball is not pitched.

The fullback fakes the Veer play. He fakes to the left and this is predetermined no matter which side the ball is pitched. This is to help the ball handling and faking to the right-handed quarterback. The fullback will fake the Veer to the right if the quarterback is left-handed. The fullback actually does the faking so the quarterback's thinking and mechanics can focus on the pitch to one of the halfbacks. The fullback's close alignment helps the timing and faking on the Quick Pitch very much. The halfbacks flare with speed to the outside, looking for the pitch. They actually gain a little depth on their flare to have a good angle to run the ball to the outside if they receive it. After receiving the pitch, the halfback reads the tackle's block and runs accordingly. The quarterback steps out, as in the Veer play, to the left. He quickly pitches with a spiral pitch to the left halfback or pivots one step back to the right and pitches the same type of pitch to the right halfback. An open end will block to the inside instead of reaching out and hook blocking (Diagram 6-5).

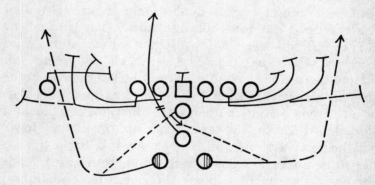

**Diagram 6-5**
**Quick Pitch**

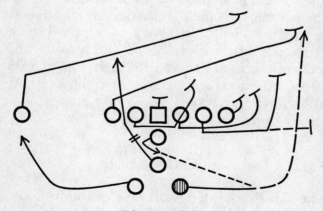

**Diagram 6-6**
**Predetermined Quick Pitch**

The only changes for the predetermined pitch involve the off side of the line. The left end and left tackle release downfield to block in the running lane with side body blocks. The left guard pulls and fill-blocks over the right guard area (Diagram 6-6).

## WIDE COUNTER DIVE

The Wide Counter Dive like the Quick Pitch lets the halfback run to the side he aligns on. It lets the halfback run off tackle. The Wide Counter Dive is unusual in several ways. It resembles a power play and has some characteristics of the outside Veer. It is a quick-hitting counter play with power.

The left end releases downfield into the running lane and executes a side body block. The left tackle also releases downfield and blocks in the running lane. The left guard, center and right guard all base block to their left. The right tackle also base blocks the men on him to the inside. The right end blocks to the inside. The fullback is a key blocker on this play by having to block the defensive end out. He does not fake to the left like the other three backs, but goes straight to a point just outside the right end's alignment to block the defensive end out with a shoulder block with his head on the ball carrier's side.

Both halfbacks jab-step to the left and start their sprint to the right. The left halfback fakes an option play to the right after the jab step. His path and action are just like the counter option. The right halfback takes a path toward the inside foot of the right end. He receives the ball and runs the hole between the blocks of the right end and fullback. The quarterback jab-steps to the left, pivots and steps to the right, handing off to the left halfback. He then continues to fake outside as he does on the counter option play (Diagram 6-7).

## CROSSBUCK

The Crossbuck is a scissors type of counter play. It can be run as a short or long type of trap play. The crossbuck is a counter from the fake of the Belly play. Diagram 6-8 shows the different paths taken on the both short and long traps of the crossbuck.

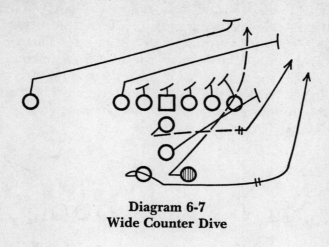

**Diagram 6-7**
**Wide Counter Dive**

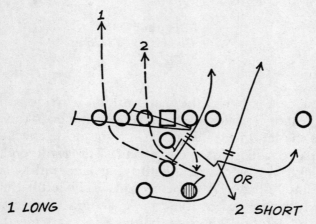

1 LONG                                    2 SHORT

**Diagram 6-8**
**Crossbuck Routes**

Player responsibilities will change at the point of attack according to the type of defense that is faced. This will affect the left end and left tackle on the long or wide Crossbuck. There are two types of situations at the point of attack. The left end will determine his block according to the number of defensive men aligned on him and to his outside. He blocks to the inside if there is only one man on him or to his outside. This type of blocking would be against the odd or Fifty-Four defense. He blocks to the outside after an influence block if there are two men on him or to his outside. This rule would apply against the split-six or split-four or even defense. The left tackle blocks the man over him or if there is no man over him, then he will block to the inside. The left guard blocks the man on him. He may have to use a come-around block against the split defense (Diagram 6-9).

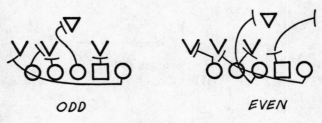

ODD                                    EVEN

**Diagram 6-9**
**Wide Crossbuck Blocking**

The center blocks the man on him, playside gap or back side in that order. The right guard pulls and traps the first man outside the left tackle's block. The right tackle check-blocks in the area of the right guard's pull. The right end releases downfield and blocks in the running lane with a side body block. The fullback fakes the veer play. The left halfback fakes the Belly play. Both of these backs should fake very hard to freeze the defense. The right halfback fakes to the right with a jab step and then he goes to the left, making a pocket to receive the handoff. His course should be toward the left tackle's outside foot. After receiving the ball he cuts upfield between the tackle's block and the trap block of the right guard. The quarterback steps out to the right and fakes the Veer to the fullback. Then he steps back and hands off to the right halfback. Then he continues to fake the Belly play to the left halfback. After this fake, he will either fake the Belly Keep outside or the Belly Pass (Diagram 6-10).

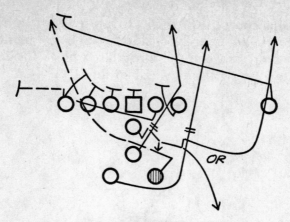

**Diagram 6-10**
**Wide Crossbuck**

The short trap used with the Crossbuck will attack the defense in the one- and three-hole area. The left tackle, left guard and center will have different assignments according to the defense that is faced. The left tackle will block inside. The left guard also will block inside. The center will block the man over him or to the back side. These assignments are simple and will remain constant. The difference is that they will block a different man against different defenses (Diagram 6-11).

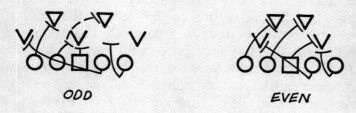

ODD                              EVEN

**Diagram 6-11**

The other player responsibilities are for the left end to release downfield and block in the running lane. The right tackle check-blocks. The right end has the same assignment as on the wide version of the Crossbuck. All the backs have the same assignments as on the wide Crossbuck. The right halfback will adjust his course on the short trap used in the Crossbuck and aim for the left guard's outside foot after receiving the ball. He cuts upfield between the left guard's block inside and the trap block of the right guard (Diagram 6-12).

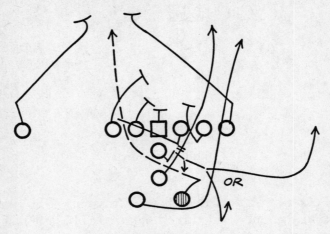

**Diagram 6-12**
**Short Crossbuck**

There is one blocking variation that is very useful to use with the Crossbuck. This is a type of isolation blocking. The combination blocking would be either Ninety-One (91) or Ninety-Three (93) according to the defense that is faced. All assignments are the same as on the short Crossbuck except that the left tackle will block out and the right guard base blocks to the right along with the right tackle. The back assignments are the same except that the left halfback will take a jab step to the right and then lead the play through the one or three hole and block the linebacker on that side. The left guard has a special rule on the isolation Crossbuck in that he blocks inside against the odd defense and blocks to the outside against an even or split defense (Diagram 6-13).

This is a useful variation if the offensive guards do not pull or trap well or if stunting in the pulling guard's area is causing trouble to the offense. Diagram 6-14 shows a detailed blocking breakdown against both the odd and even defenses at the point of attack for the isolation blocking pattern of the Crossbuck variation.

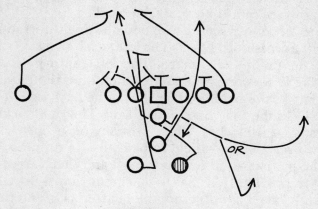

**Diagram 6-13**
**Crossbuck Variation**

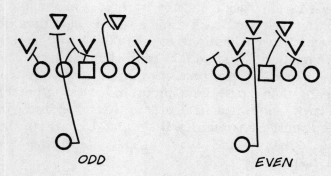

*ODD*                    *EVEN*

**Diagram 6-14**

## FULLBACK TRAP

Many Wishbone teams do not use trap blocking in their plan of attack. There is a definite place for trap blocking in the Multiple Wishbone attack. The trap blocking scheme is different to the defense and causes problems to the defense since most Wishbone blocking is base or straight ahead blocking. The defense looks for the straight ahead block and is surprised by the trap block. This can result in the big gainer. It is especially true since the fullback is aligned close and can hit into the secondary very quickly with a trap block.

The left end releases to block downfield in the running lane with a cross-body block. The left tackle check-blocks in the area of the pulling left guard. The left guard pulls and trap blocks the first defensive man outside of the right guard. The center blocks the man over him or to the back side. The right guard blocks the first man to his inside. The right tackle blocks inside as a seal blocker. This is usually on a linebacker. The right end releases downfield to block in the running lane.

The halfbacks jab-step to the left and then carry out fakes to the right. The left halfback comes across to the right, receiving a fake handoff from the quarterback, and then fakes up into the off-tackle area. The fullback starts a Veer fake to the left, receives the ball and bends back over the outside foot of the center. He runs the lane created by the blocking of the center, right guard, right tackle and the trap block of the left guard. The quarterback steps back using a shorter step than he does on the Veer play. He hands off to the fullback with his left hand and then continues back to fake to the left halfback. Then the quarterback will drop on back two more steps, pivot quickly around and fake a pass. One important coaching point is that the fullback will run a straighter course after receiving the handoff against even defenses. Diagram 6-15 shows the internal blocking variations and Diagram 6-16 shows the complete fullback trap.

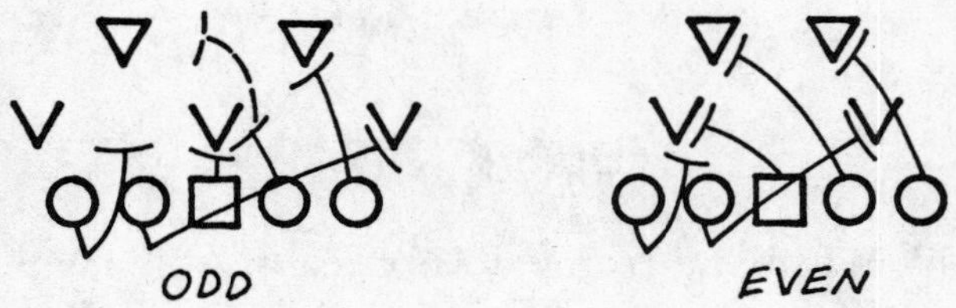

ODD                  EVEN

**Diagram 6-15**
**Internal Blocking**

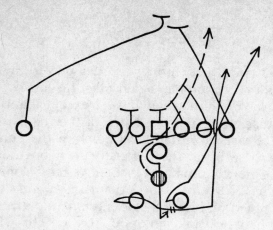

**Diagram 6-16**
**Fullback Trap**

The fullback trap can be executed with a full flow fake with the backs if desired. All line assignments remain the same. The halfbacks will fake an option to the left. The quarterback also fakes an option to the left after handing off to the fullback. The fullback has the same assignment. This fullback trap variation will be very effective against defenses that pursue fast toward flow (Diagram 6-17).

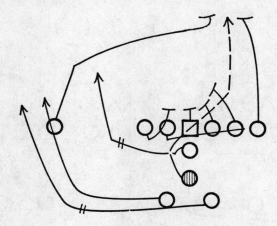

**Diagram 6-17**
**Fullback Trap Variation**

## VEER CUTBACK

This is the quickest hitting counter play in the Wishbone offense. It is a very good play against fast-flowing defenses. The play should look like the regular Veer except that the fullback makes a cutback after the third step of the regular Veer path. Both ends release downfield and block in the running lane. The tackles base block the defensive men on them to their outside. The guards also base block the defensive men on them to the outside. The center blocks the man on him to the left. If no one is aligned on him, he blocks the man on the back side. Both of the halfbacks fake an option to the right. The fullback takes a Veer course for three steps, receives the handoff and cuts back over the right guard-center gap. The quarterback fakes an option after handing off to the fullback.

Note that a linebacker is left unblocked against the split defense. This may look unsound but the flow fake will take the linebacker out of the play and the cutback hits so fast that the linebacker cannot recover in time to be in one the play. Players will have to see this work on the practice field to believe that this is true and have confidence in the play. Diagram 6-18 shows the cutback against both the odd and even defenses.

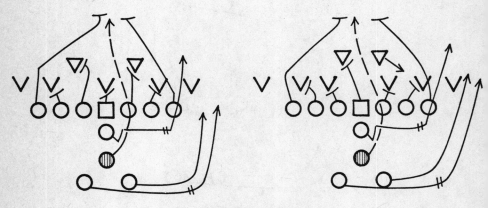

**Diagram 6-18**
**Veer Cutback**

## SPEED

This is a special Veer variation that is excellent against the stack gap defense. This is a good automatic play for the quarterback to check off when he sees the gap stack defense and there is a normal down and distance to go. The ends release and block downfield in the running lane. The left tackle blocks the man on him with a base block to the left. The left guard and the right tackle can help block on the stacked linebackers or check-block the men shooting the gaps. A coaching point is to take good splits when running the play. The center and right guard block the linebackers on their respective sides. The fullback aligns closer to the quarterback by moving up one foot. He shifts up after the quarterback calls the speed play as an automatic. He runs the center guard gap on the wide side of the stack. The fullback's close alignment, the quickness of the play hitting the line and the large splits will get the ball carrier past the shooting gap men without their having to be blocked. The halfbacks fake wide as they do on the option

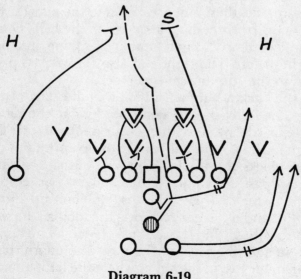

**Diagram 6-19**
**Speed**

play. The quarterback steps out with a shorter step than he uses on the Veer play and hands off to the diving fullback. He fakes an option after the handoff (Diagram 6-19).

## DRAW

There are several draw plays that can be executed in the Multiple Wishbone offense. The draw play that is used should fit the personnel, formations that are used and complement the type of passing attack that is being used.

The draw discussed here can be run from the regular Wishbone, Pro or Twins formations. This is because both of the ends are able to execute their assignments from any position. It is also true for the right halfback. This draw is executed from the sprint out pass fake because the sprint out passing attack blends in well with the Multiple Wishbone concept. The left halfback runs the ball because he is one of the best runners.

The left end sprints downfield, executing a pass cut, and then gets into the running lane to block. All the internal linemen fire out aggressively to block. Then they maintain contact and work their defensive man to the outside away from the left guard or three-hole area where the ball is going to be run. The left guard has an option of taking his man either way—right or left. The right end also runs a pass pattern and then gets to the running lane to block.

All the back assignments look like the start of the sprint out pass. The fullback shows pass blocking to the right for one or two steps, delays and then leads the ball carrier up the running lane. The right halfback runs his sprint out pass route and then blocks downfield. The left halfback sprints to the right, shows pass blocking and then makes a pocket for the ball. He will be facing the right with his left elbow up and the palm of his right hand up. After receiving the football, he will run for daylight, reading the left guard's block. The quarterback sprints out, showing pass all the way. The quarterback comes back at an angle just to the left of where the left halfback sets up showing his pass block. As he approaches the left halfback, he takes the ball into his left hand and lowers it into the pocket made by the left halfback. This mesh is made by the quarterback coming close to the left halfback. They should actually touch shoulder pads lightly as they pass one another. The quarterback continues to fake the sprint out pass after making the handoff to the left halfback (Diagram 6-20).

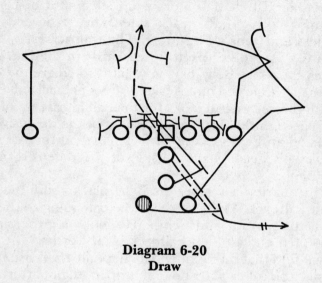

**Diagram 6-20**
**Draw**

## BELLY PASS

The Belly Pass is a good complementary play to the basic Belly play and the Belly Keep Outside. The play becomes very difficult for the defense because the quarterback can make it into an option pass or run play. The Belly Pass has the good feature of getting the fullback out as a pass receiver and using the right halfback as a blocker. This serves two advantages. Most offensive teams do not use their fullback as a receiver. Defensive secondary men will have more trouble spotting him as a receiver since he is hidden by his close alignment and he comes out as a receiver from the middle of the formation. The right halfback is in good position to block the defensive end. His block on the end will also serve as a key breaker on the defensive secondary.

The left end runs a runs a streak route through the safety area to freeze the back side of the defensive secondary. All internal linemen use regular pass blocking by firing out aggressively as in a running play. Then they make contact and keep their defensive man tied up. Uncovered linemen will pick up stunts or blitzes. The uncovered left guard or center will drop and block on the back side. The right end releases downfield and runs a flag route. The fullback fakes the Veer and runs a flat route five to seven yards in the flat. The left halfback fakes the Belly play very hard to freeze the defense. He tries to get tackled on his fake. If he is not tackled, he hooks as a dump receiver and looks for the ball in case no one else is open. The right halfback goes straight at the defensive end as he does on an Eighty-Six (86) block. Then at the last moment he drives his head to the outside of the defensive man and blocks him in.

The quarterback fakes the Belly play to both the fullback and left halfback. Then he keeps the ball going to the outside while getting width and depth. He looks for the right end, fullback, left end and left halfback in that order. The quarterback will find that the right end or the fullback is usually open; especially the fullback. If no one is open, the quarterback yells "run" and runs the football. The receivers peel back to block when the quarterback yells "run" (Diagram 6-21).

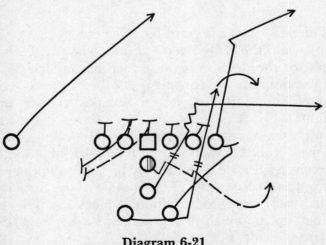

**Diagram 6-21**
**Belly Pass**

## HALFBACK PASS

The Halfback Pass is a good complementary play to the option or triple option. The left end has the same route as he does on the Belly Pass—a streak route through the safety area. All the internal linemen use regular pass blocking as they do for the Belly Pass. The right end releases to the outside as he does on the triple option. Then he sprints downfield faking a block at the defender on him before cutting out on a flag route. The fullback and the right halfback execute the same assignment as they do on the Belly Pass. The quarterback uses the same mechanics as he does on the option and pitches to the left halfback two steps after the fake to the fullback. Then he helps the right halfback with his block on the defensive end. The left halfback starts to the right as he does on the option play, receives the pitch from the quarterback and looks for the right end, fullback or left end in that order. He will adjust the ball immediately after receiving the pitch so he can be ready to pass as the receiver begins to break open in the secondary. He also will be getting width so he can execute the option pass run. He calls "run" if no receiver is open and runs the ball. The receivers peel back and block if they hear the left halfback call "run." The

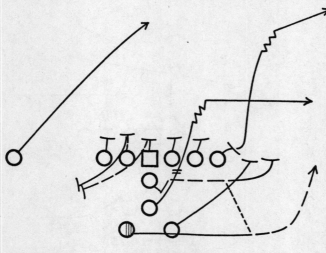

**Diagram 6-22**
**Halfback Pass**

whole play should look like the option or triple option until the last moment (Diagram 6-22).

## ROLL PASS

The Roll Pass is a companion play to the counter dive. It has some aspects of the bootleg blended into it. There are three receivers on one side of the field so the quarterback has an easier choice to pick the open receiver. The option of running with the football is present if no one is open. The left end runs a cross route. He is halfway between the other two receivers in depth. All the internal linemen carry out regular pass blocking by firing out aggressively into the men on them and keeping contact. The right end releases downfield to block just as he does on the counter dive play. He is reading the deep defensive man to his side. He cuts to the right when he determines that he can beat the defensive back on the cut to the outside. This route is just like the in-and-out route used with the bootleg pass.

The fullback fakes the Veer and releases five to seven yards into the right flat. The left halfback fakes the counter dive very hard to freeze the defense. The right halfback takes the first two steps of the counter option and goes to the right and blocks the defensive end. He goes straight toward the end

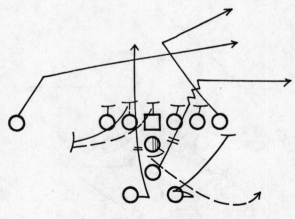

**Diagram 6-23**
**Roll Pass**

and gets his head to the outside and blocks the defensive end in. The quarterback fakes to the fullback and left halfback just as he does in the counter dive, but will keep the ball, hiding it in the faking pocket. He then sprints to the right getting width and depth and looking for the open receiver. He looks for the right end first, the left end second, and the fullback third. Again the fullback will be open a lot since he is not seen by the defense as he releases into the flat (Diagram 6-23).

## SCREEN

The Screen that is used should be designed to fit personnel and formations. This screen is really a triple screen in that it has three receivers: the quarterback can read the defense and throw to the open receiver. This screen can also be executed with a predetermined receiver, and also can be executed from broken bone formations.

The ends release downfield on pass routes and then peel back to block downfield in the running lane. The left tackle, left guard and center execute screen blocks by firing out aggressively for two counts. Then they pull to the left. The left tackle goes four yards and pivots back to the inside to block. The left guard goes three yards beyond the left tackle and blocks to the outside. The center pulls through the lane and blocks downfield. If the center thinks or is told that the middle screen is coming, he stays and blocks in the middle. The right guard and right tackle fire out and block aggressively for three counts. Then they fake being beaten on their blocks. They release downfield to block when the fullback calls "block."

The fullback fakes the Veer and then sets up to receive the ball just in the center-right guard gap. If he receives the ball, he calls "block" and runs to daylight downfield. The left halfback sprints to the right, stops four yards deep behind the right tackle's alignment and sets up to block. He blocks for three counts and then slips out into the right flat to be the third or outlet receiver. The right halfback takes one step up and sprints to the left to set up to receive the ball about five yards outside the left tackle's original alignment. The quarterback fakes the

Veer and drops quickly to set up, getting plenty of depth. On his drop he quickly fakes a pass at seven yards and then continues to drop back. He looks to the left for the right halfback first, the fullback in the middle, second and the left halfback in the right flat, third. Diagram 6-24.

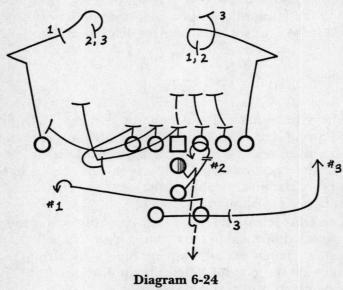

**Diagram 6-24**
**Screen**

# CHAPTER 7

## Coaching the Wishbone Power Series

The Wishbone alignment is the best in football to execute the power or isolation series. This is because the Wishbone alignment is a balanced formation. There is no indication by alignment as to where the ball is going to be run as in the Power I formation. The defense must play with a balanced defense since the Wishbone is a balanced offensive formation. Otherwise, the defense has a weakness that can be easily recognized and attacked. The close positioning of the backs makes it easy for the backs to execute double-team blocks. The alignment is also good for timing of the quarterback's handoff and the runners hitting their holes properly.

The power series is effective with small quick backs, larger slower power runners, or a combination of the two. The power series is good in bad weather (rain, mud and snow). It is also good in short-yardage situations and as a goal-line offense.

The power series gives the defense the added problem of how to deal with double-team blocks along with one-on-one and combination blocking used with other Wishbone series.

### POWER OPTION

The Power Option has the run-to-daylight option for the ball carrier. The left end releases downfield to block in the running lane. The left tackle will fire out into the defensive man on him for one count and then release to block downfield in the running lane. The left guard, center and right guard all base block to the left. The right tackle blocks the man on him either in or out. His first choice is to block to the inside. The right end blocks either out or in. His first choice is to block out on the defensive end. He also experiments on his split and will split out as far as the man on his outside will go and still stay aligned outside. This flex can be up to 15 feet. The right end must stay with his block. Form is important in staying with the block.

The fullback and right halfback will come together for their double-team block and block the defensive man that the right end does not. They take short steps and align their shoulders together to execute their block. The left halfback starts to his right, making a pocket to receive the football. After receiving the ball, he looks for his opening from the inside out. The hole to run may be outside the right guard, outside the right tackle or outside the right end. The quarterback pivots to his left, taking a drop step to get depth to make his handoff to the left halfback. After making the handoff, he fakes a bootleg or keep pass (Diagram 7-1).

The power series can be predetermined to hit any hole along the line of scrimmage. All the plays will start out alike, but end up at different holes along the line of scrimmage.

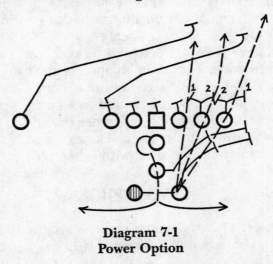

**Diagram 7-1**
**Power Option**

## ZERO-HOLE POWER PLAY

The Zero-Hole Power Play is a quick-hitter with double-team blocks along with good blocking angles. The left end releases downfield to block in the running lane. The left tackle base blocks to the left. The left guard blocks the man on him to the left with a base block. The center blocks any man over him to the left. If no man is on the center, he will block back side. The right guard blocks out against the split defense and in against the odd defense. This will give a double-team block with the center against the odd defense. The right tackle base blocks to the right. The right end releases downfield to block in the running lane. The fullback and right halfback step together to block the linebacker on their side with a double-team shoulder block. The left halfback takes one step to the right, receives the football and cuts for the center's right foot, and adjusts his running course according to the path that is opened. The quarterback pivots to the left, taking a drop step to gain depth to make his handoff to the left halfback. He will then fade to the left as much as possible to allow the left halfback a better angle to approach the hole. The quarterback fakes a bootleg to the left after handing off to the left halfback (Diagrams 7-2 and 7-3).

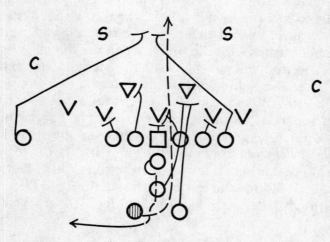

**Diagram 7-2**
**Zero Power Play Against an Odd Defense**

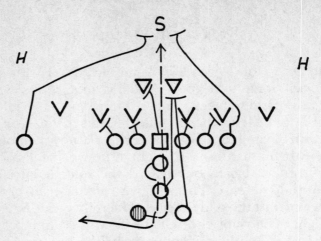

**Diagram 7-3**
**Zero-Hole Power Play Against a Split Defense**

## TWO-HOLE POWER PLAY

The left end blocks downfield in the blocking lane along with the left tackle after he blocks the man on him for one count before releasing. The left guard and center base block to the left. The right guard and right tackle will double-team block the defensive man aligned on the right guard. The right end will block inside on a linebacker against a split defense and outside against an odd defense. The fullback and right half-back double-team block the first man on the line of scrimmage outside the double-team block of the right guard and right tackle. They use a double-team shoulder block.

The left halfback takes two steps to the right, receives the football and runs a course between the right guard and right tackle's original alignment. The quarterback pivots to his left, taking a drop step to gain depth, and hands off to the left halfback. He then fakes a keep pass to the right. The quarterback will not fade to the left as he did on the Zero Play, but will come straight back to make the handoff (Diagrams 7-4 and 7-5).

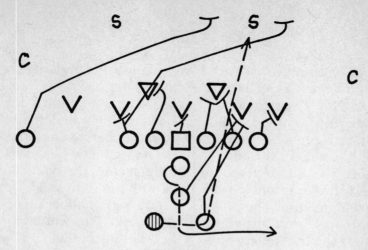

**Diagram 7-4**
**Two-Hole Power Play Against an Odd Defense**

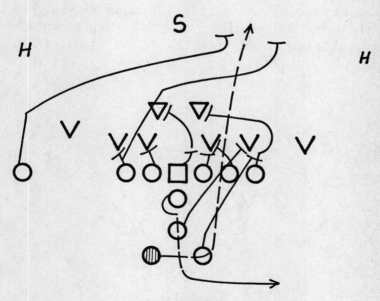

**Diagram 7-5**
**Two-Hole Power Play Against a Split Defense**

## FOUR-HOLE POWER PLAY

The Four-Hole Power Play has the same blocking for the left end, left tackle, left guard and center as in the Two-Hole Power Play. The right guard blocks the man over him to the left. He may use a come-around block against the split defense. The right tackle blocks inside against the split defense and the man over him against the odd defen'e. The right end blocks outside against the split defense and inside against the odd defense. This will give a double-team block with the right tackle against the odd defense. The fullback and the right halfback block the first man outside the right tackle's block. This will be an end against the odd defense and a tackle or linebacker against the split defense. They execute a double shoulder block. The left halfback goes to the right two steps, receives the handoff, takes one more step and cuts off the right tackle's outside foot. The quarterback pivots back to the left and gets depth to make the handoff to the left halfback. He will angle to the right more than he did on the Two-Hole Power Play. After the handoff, the quarterback fakes a keep pass to the right (Diagrams 7-6 and 7-7).

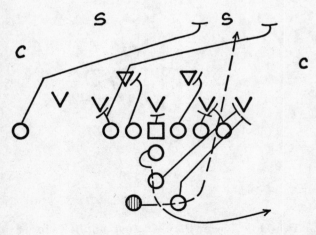

**Diagram 7-6**
**Four-Hole Power Play Against an Odd Defense**

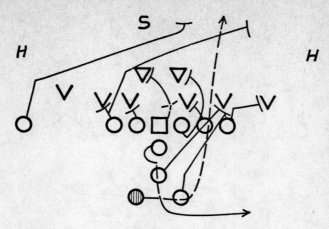

**Diagram 7-7**
**Four-Hole Power Play Against a Split Defense**

## SIX-HOLE POWER PLAY

The Six-Hole Power Play has the same blocking as the Two- and Four-Hole Power Plays for the left end, left tackle, left guard, center and right guard. The right tackle blocks inside against the split defense and double-teams with the end against

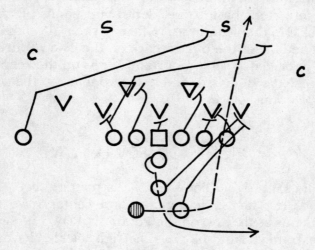

**Diagram 7-8**
**Six-Hole Power Play Against an Odd Defense**

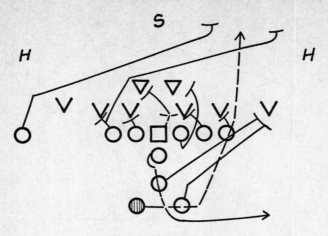

**Diagram 7-9**
**Six-Hole Power Play Against a Split Defense**

the odd defense. The right end double-team blocks to the inside against the odd defense and single blocks to the inside against the split defense. The fullback and right halfback double-team block together on the defensive end with a double shoulder block. The left halfback starts to the right, receives the football and takes two more steps before cutting off the right end's outside foot on his path upfield. The quarterback pivots to the left, steps back to get depth and hands off to the left halfback. He then continues to fake to the right, faking a keep pass. The fake of the quarterback on the Two-, Four- and Six-Hole Power Play is very important. It sets up the keep pass and will freeze the defensive end and secondary to the side of the fake (Diagrams 7-8 and 7-9).

## EIGHT-HOLE POWER PLAY

The Eight-Hole Power Play is a power sweep. Again the left end, left tackle, left guard and center have the same assignments as they do on the Power-Six Play. The right guard base or come-around blocks. The right tackle blocks the man over him or to the inside. The right end blocks to the inside. The fullback and the right halfback approach the defensive end as they do on the Six-Hole Power Play as if they are going to block him out. They both make contact and then the fullback slips off and sprints to the outside to block the first man to show in the flat. The right halfback stays with the defensive end and uses a shoulder block to take him in. If the defensive end starts to escape, the right halfback goes down on all fours (hands and feet) and scramble blocks, keeping the defensive end's legs tied up so he cannot escape to the outside. The quarterback reverse pivots and pitches the football to the left halfback and then leads the ball carrier upfield to block. The left halfback sprints to the right, receives the pitch and cuts upfield outside the right halfback's block (Diagram 7-10).

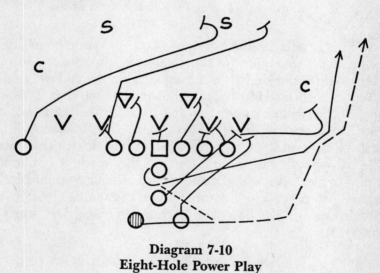

**Diagram 7-10**
**Eight-Hole Power Play**

The Eight-Hole Power Play is good to run into the split end side of the offense. Blocking assignments change for three players. The fullback will block the first man outside the right tackle. The right halfback blocks the defensive end. The split end will release downfield for about four yards, come under control and shield block on any defensive man coming from the inside. If no pursuit comes from the inside, he will look on downfield to block (Diagram 7-11).

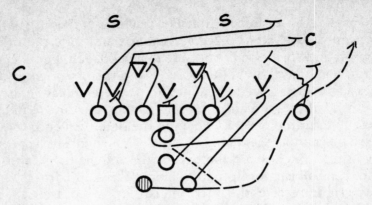

**Diagram 7-11**
**Eight-Hole Power Play to the Split End**

The predetermined power plays are very good for the goal-line offense and in short-yardage situations. Only one adjustment is needed to block against the Sixty-Five goal-line defense that is used by most teams on the goal line. This is the block by the fullback and right halfback. Instead of the double-team block, they will block individually. The fullback will block to the inside and the right halfback will block to the outside. The play is called in the huddle and the words "Goal line" are added to alert the fullback and right halfback to their blocking change. All other assignments remain the same. The left tackle will also stay on the line of scrimmage to block (Diagrams 7-12 and 7-13).

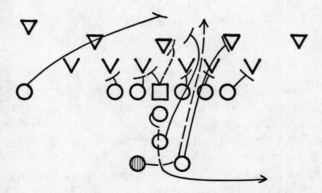

**Diagram 7-12**
**Two-Hole Power Play with Goal-Line Adjustment**

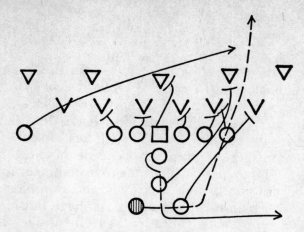

**Diagram 7-13**
**Four-Hole Power Play With Goal-Line Adjustment**

## POWER FOUR-KEEP EIGHT

This is a good play with a strong fake inside, with the ball being run outside. All the linemen have the same assignments as they do on the Eight-Hole Power Play. The fullback and right halfback also have the same assignment. The only change is that the quarterback fakes giving the football to the left halfback as he fakes a Four-Hole Power Play. Then the quarterback sprints to the outside and cuts upfield (Diagram 7-14).

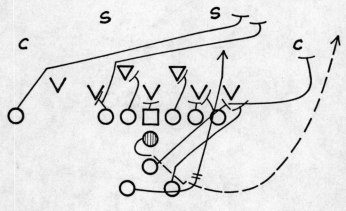

**Diagram 7-14**
**Power Four-Keep Eight**

## POWER COUNTER

This is the only counter play used in the Power Series. Combination blocking is used. Twenty-Five blocking is used against the odd defense and Twenty-Three blocking is used against the split defense. The left end releases downfield to side body block in the running lane. The left tackle blocks inside on the linebacker. The left guard blocks inside on or off the line of scrimmage. The center will block the man on him or to the back side. The right guard pulls to the left and trap blocks on the first defensive man on the line of scrimmage outside the left guard. The right tackle check-blocks to his inside. The right end releases downfield to block in the running lane.

The fullback starts to the right just as he does on the Four-Hole Power Play and blocks the first defensive man to show just outside the right tackle. The left halfback fakes a Four-Hole Power Play. The right halfback takes a counter step to the right and then aims at the center's left foot. He receives the football from the quarterback on an inside handoff. His left elbow will be up. He adjusts his run according to the combination

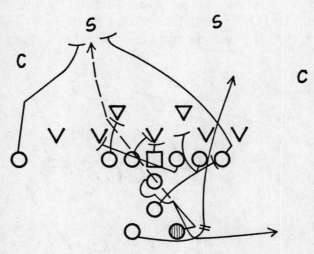

**Diagram 7-15**
**Power Counter with Twenty-Five Blocking**

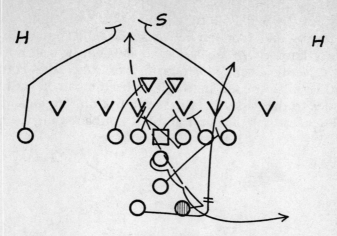

**Diagram 7-16**
**Power Counter with Twenty-Three Blocking**

blocking that is called. The quarterback pivots on his right foot and opens to the right more than on the regular power plays. He makes an inside handoff to the right halfback with his left hand. Then he gains depth and fakes a Power Four Play to the left halfback. After this fake, the quarterback fakes a Power Keep Pass to the right (Diagrams 7-15 and 7-16).

## POWER KEEP PASS

The Power Keep Pass comes off the Four-Hole Power Play fake. This is because the mesh of the left halfback and quarterback on their fake allows the quarterback to move to the outside to pass more quickly than the fakes on the other power plays. The left end runs a drag route seven to nine yards deep. The internal linemen carry out regular pass protection blocking with all the linemen firing out aggressively on their blocks and keeping contact with their men. The uncovered left guard or center drops back to block on the back side. The right end fakes a block to the inside and then releases on a flag route.

The fullback and right halfback go at the defensive end as they do on the Four-Hole Power Play. They both make contact and then the fullback slips off into the flat, five yards deep, looking for the ball. The right halfback stays with his block on the defensive end. The left halfback fakes the Four-Hole Power Play very hard. If he does not get tackled, he will hook as a safety valve receiver. The quarterback fakes the Four-Hole Power Play with the left halfback, hides the ball on his hip and continues to the right for a pass-run option. He looks for the right end, fullback, left end and left halfback in that order. If

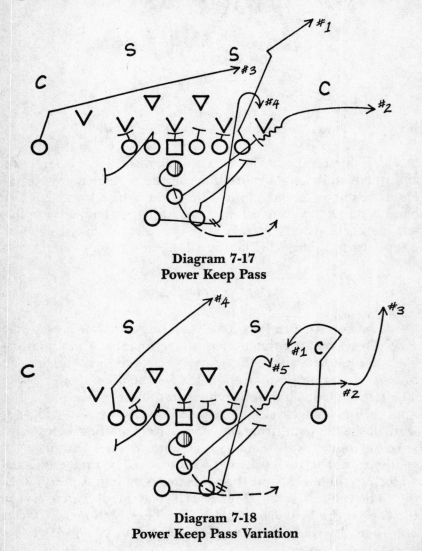

**Diagram 7-17**
**Power Keep Pass**

**Diagram 7-18**
**Power Keep Pass Variation**

no receiver is open, the quarterback calls "Block" and runs the football. Using the fullback as a receiver is good for he is hidden from the defensive secondary by his close alignment and by being in the center of the offense. (Diagram 7-17).

A good variation is to run the Power Keep pass into the split end side. The only change is for the ends and fullback. The left end will run a streak route through the safety area. The split end will execute a curl route about ten to 12 yards deep. The fullback still has the flat route but will turn upfield if he runs too close to the sideline on his flat route (Diagram 7-18).

## POWER BOOTLEG

The Power Bootleg comes off the Four-Hole Power Play fake. The left end executes an in-and-out route. The left tackle will reach-block on the defensive tackle. The left guard blocks the man over him. The center blocks the man over him or to the back side. The right guard pulls to the left, looking to block the defensive end either in or out. He will prefer to block him in. The right tackle checks with a block in the area where the right guard pulled from. The right end runs a drag route seven to nine yards deep. The fullback and the right halfback come together to block as they do on a Four-Hole Power Play. Then the fullback slips off and runs a bend route down the middle. He is quite open if he can clear the line of scrimmage without getting knocked down. This is because he is hidden from the defensive secondary by his alignment in the middle. Defensive secondary men look at and key ends and halfbacks mostly. The right halfback blocks the first defensive man to show outside the right tackle's block. The left halfback fakes a Four-Hole Power Play. He then continues to cut out into the deep right flat for a possible throwback pass.

The quarterback fakes to the left halfback as he does on the Four-Hole Power Play and then levels out, sprinting to the left and hiding the football on his hip. As he comes to the left, he reads the block of the right guard. If the guard blocks in, the quarterback goes outside. If the guard blocks out, the quarterback pulls up short to throw. The quarterback looks for the left

end first, the right end second, the fullback third and possibly
the left halfback fourth. If any receiver finds himself open on a
previously run Power Bootleg, he tells the quarterback and the
quarterback can make him the primary receiver the next time
the pass is run (Diagram 7-19).

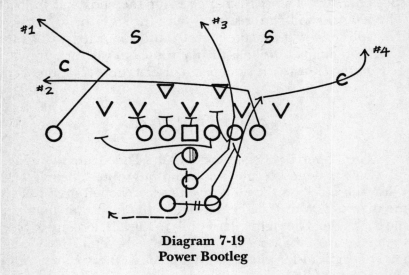

**Diagram 7-19**
**Power Bootleg**

The Power Bootleg can be run using the Eight-Hole Power
Play fake. This involves a change in assignments for only two
men. The quarterback now quickly pitches to the left halfback.
Then he starts a path back as he does on the regular bootleg.
He will receive a handoff from the left halfback as he gets depth
and passes by the left halfback. The left halfback will now take a
counter step so he will not receive the ball too far to the right.
He receives the pitch, takes one or two steps to the right and
then makes a handoff back to the quarterback with his left
hand. Then he fakes the Eight-Hole Power Play (Diagram
7-20).

The Power Bootleg may also be run with the ends changing assignments. All other assignments remain the same. This is
a good play on the goal line or third down. The left end runs a
quick flat route and looks for the ball immediately. He will run a
depth to insure the first down or touchdown. The quarterback
must be prepared to deliver the ball as soon as the left end is
open (Diagram 7-21).

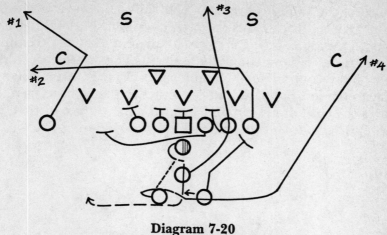

**Diagram 7-20**
**Power Bootleg Variation**

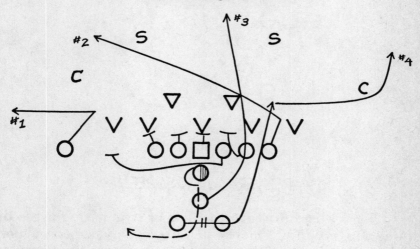

**Diagram 7-21**
**Power Bootleg Quick**

## POWER COUNTER PASS

The Power Counter Pass is a companion play to the Power
Counter. It is good to use when the Power Counter has been
run several times effectively. The left end runs a cross route
halfway between the right end's and fullback's depth. This will
be approximately ten to eleven yards deep. All the internal
linemen have regular pass protection blocking. The right end

executes an in-and-out route. The fullback runs a flat route. The right halfback fakes the power counter. The left halfback goes to the right faking a Four-Hole Power Play and continues to the right to block the defensive end. The quarterback fakes the power counter to the right halfback, a Four-Hole Power Play to the left halfback and continues to the right to pass. He hides the ball on his hip and looks for the right end first, the left end second and the fullback third (Diagram 7-22).

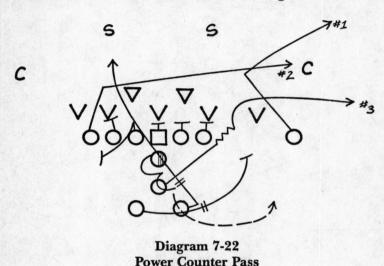

**Diagram 7-22**
**Power Counter Pass**

## POWER QUICK SCREEN

The left end drives off the line of scrimmage for two or three steps very fast. Then he steps back to his aligned position to receive the pass. The left tackle, left guard and center execute screen blocking by firing out one count and then pulling to the left to block. The left tackle blocks back to the inside, the left guard to the outside and the center pulls upfield to block. The right guard and right tackle base block. The right end also base blocks. The fullback and right halfback double-team block to the right as they do on the Four-Hole Power Play. The left halfback fakes a Four-Hole Power Play. The quarterback fakes a handoff to the left halfback and quickly throws to the left end (Diagram 7-23).

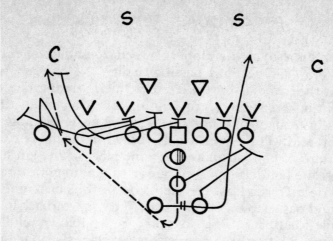

**Diagram 7-23**
**Power Quick Screen**

A quicker method of delivering the quick screen is for the quarterback to fake a pitch to the left halfback as he does on the Eight-Hole Power Play. Then he quickly turns and delivers the ball to the left end. All other assignments remain the same as on the Power Quick Screen (Diagram 7-24).

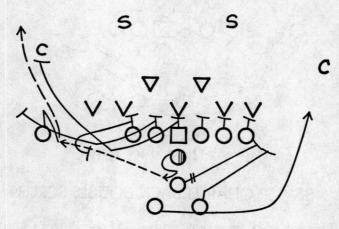

**Diagram 7-24**
**Power Quick Screen Variation**

## POWER QUARTERBACK SCREEN

This is a slower-developing screen. It is an excellent screen if the left halfback has passing ability. All line assignments remain the same as on the Power Quick Screen. The pulling screen blockers will hold their initial blocking contact for two counts instead of one, for this is a slower-developing screen. The left end will now release downfield to block. The fullback and the right halfback have the same blocks. The left halfback receives the handoff and continues to the right as he does on an Eight-Hole Power Play. He then stops, drops back one or two steps and passes to the quarterback. The quarterback hands off to the left halfback as he does on a Four-Hole Power Play and fakes to the left as in a bootleg. He executes a poor fake and then sets up to receive the screen pass from the left halfback. The positioning of the left halfback and the quarterback is such that the pass is a forward one (Diagram 7-25).

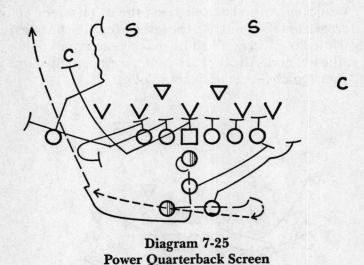

**Diagram 7-25**
**Power Quarterback Screen**

## POWER QUARTERBACK DOUBLE SCREEN

This is a trick type play coming off the Power Quarterback Screen. It must be set up by successfully executing the Power Quarterback Screen. The left end sprints downfield, fakes a block and then runs a deep flag route. The left tackle, left guard and center start their screen blocks, but pull up short and form a cup to protect the quarterback as he passes downfield. The right guard and right tackle base block. The right end blocks for two counts and then runs a deep drag route to the left. The fullback runs the same post route as he does on the Power Bootleg. The right halfback blocks to the right. The left halfback executes the same as he does on the Power Quarterback Screen. The quarterback also executes the same as he does on the Power Quarterback Screen until after he receives the pass from the left halfback. Then he immediately looks downfield to pass to the left end first, the right end second, and the fullback third (Diagram 7-26).

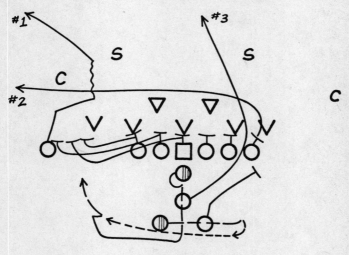

Diagram 7-26
**Power Quarterback Double Screen**

# CHAPTER 8

# *Developing the Wishbone Outside Veer*

The Wishbone is famous for its triple option using the Inside Veer. The Wishbone is also a good formation from which to run the Outside Veer. Combining the Inside Veer and the Outside Veer puts a great deal of pressure on any defense. Running both the Inside Veer and the Outside Veer from one formation will increase the effectiveness of both series. A comparison of the attacking areas and the path of the backs is shown in Diagrams 8-1 and 8-2.

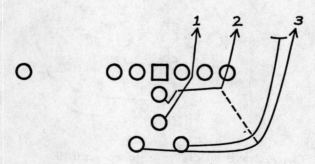

**Diagram 8-1**
**Inside Veer Attacking Areas**

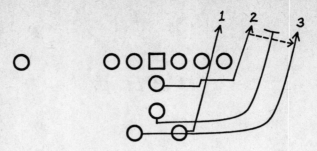

**Diagram 8-2**
**Outside Veer Attacking Areas**

The Outside Veer series attacks the defense wider than the Inside Veer. The Outside Veer combined with the Inside Veer will upset defensive responsibilities. Most defensive ends' assignment on any option play is to take the quarterback. The defense cannot assign the end to take the quarterback on the Outside Veer. If this happens, the give to the diving right halfback will always be open (Diagram 8-3).

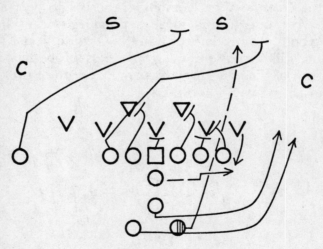

**Diagram 8-3**
**Destroying Defensive Responsibilities**

The corner is usually given the responsibility of containing the pitch man on the option. The Outside Veer creates a two-on-one situation for the corner (Diagram 8-4).

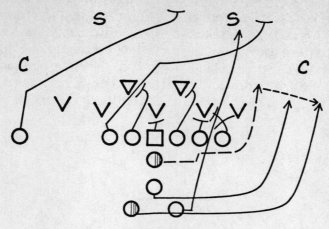

**Diagram 8-4**
**Destroying Defensive Responsibilities**

## OUTSIDE VEER DIVE

The Outside Veer Dive is predetermined and is called as such in the huddle. The left end releases to block downfield with a side body block in the running lane. The left tackle also releases downfield to block in the running lane. The left guard and center will base block to their left. The onside of the line will combination block with either a Forty-Six or Twenty-Six block (Diagram 8-5).

**Diagram 8-5**
**Combination Blocking for the Outside Veer Dive**

The fullback drop-steps one step with his right foot and runs toward the sideline until he reaches a point three yards outside the offensive end. He then turns upfield to block. The left halfback sprints to the right on a regular option course. The right halfback takes a six-inch jab step to the right and dives for the outside foot of the right tackle. He receives the football and adjusts his course to run off the right end's block. The quarterback steps down the line, reaching the handoff mesh on his third step. He hands off to the right halfback, and then continues on down the line for two steps, and cuts upfield, faking the pitch to the trailing left halfback (Diagram 8-6).

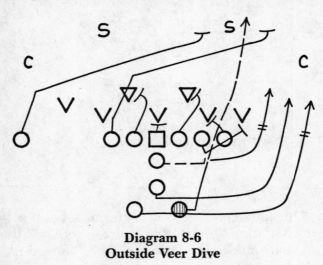

**Diagram 8-6**
**Outside Veer Dive**

## OUTSIDE VEER OPTION

The Outside Veer Option is a quarterback run or pitch option after a fake to the diving right halfback. The left end and left tackle both release and block downfield just as they do in the Outside Veer Dive except that they will try to get a hole wider to execute their blocks. The left guard and center both base block to their left. The right tackle and right end both will base block to the inside. The fullback drop-steps one step with his right foot and runs toward the sideline until he reaches a point three yards outside the offensive end. He then turns upfield to block. He is responsible for blocking the contain man.

The left halfback sprints to the right on an option course. He will keep the proper pitch position from the quarterback and look for the pitch at any time. The right halfback runs a

Veer dive path faking very hard. He strives to get tackled on his fake. The quarterback steps down the line three steps, faking to the right halfback. He then options the first defensive man to show after the fake to the right halfback. This may be the end or a cornerback. The pitch will be quick if the defensive end closes on him or will be upfield if the cornerback closes on him (Diagram 8-7).

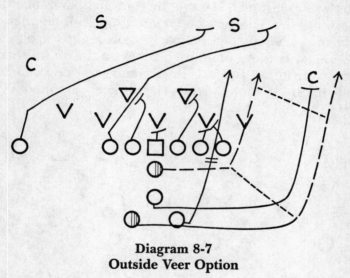

**Diagram 8-7**
**Outside Veer Option**

## OUTSIDE VEER TRIPLE OPTION

The Outside Veer Dive and the Outside Veer Option are combined in the Outside Veer Triple Option. All the linemen have the same blocks as they do in the Outside Veer Option. The fullback takes the same path but he now blocks the man responsible for the deep third of the defense. The left halfback has the same responsibility as he does on the Outside Veer Option. The right halfback and quarterback have adjustments to make when running the triple portion of the Outside Veer. The right halfback runs the same dive course as he does in the Outside Veer Dive and makes a good pocket to receive the football. He feels the ball and if it is left with him, he tightens down on the ball to run with it. He keeps his head up and can usually see if the defensive situation will allow the quarterback to give the ball or keep it.

The quarterback steps down the line, meshing with the right halfback on the third step. He puts the ball in the right halfback's pocket, reading the defensive end. If the defensive end does not close on the right halfback, he gives the ball to him. If the defensive end closes on the right halfback, the quarterback pulls the ball from the right halfback's pocket and runs around the defensive end, cutting upfield. He then looks to keep or pitch to the left halfback according to the play of the contain man. If the contain man closes on the quarterback, he pitches to the left halfback. If the contain man stays wide to play the left halfback, the quarterback will keep the football (Diagram 8-8).

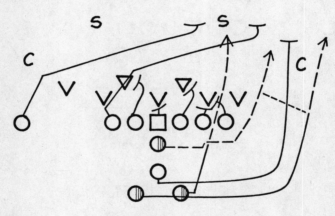

**Diagram 8-8**
**Outside Veer Triple Option**

## OUTSIDE VEER COUNTER

Defenses must flow fast to try to stop the dive, option and triple option of the Outside Veer. This will set up and make the counter play very effective. The left end releases downfield to block in the running lane with a side body block. The internal linemen all base block unless a blocking variation is called. The left tackle and left guard block to the left and the center, right guard and right tackle block to the right. The right end releases downfield and blocks in the running lane just as the left end does.

The left halfback fakes a regular option. The right halfback fakes a Veer dive very hard over the right tackle's outside foot. The fullback drop-steps with his right foot as he does on the dive, option and triple option. He then pivots, driving back to the line of scrimmage low and hard. He hits the left side of the center and adjusts his course according to the blocking that is called. The quarterback steps out two steps to the right, pivots and comes back to the left to hand off to the fullback. He then drops quickly back to fake a pass (Diagram 8-9).

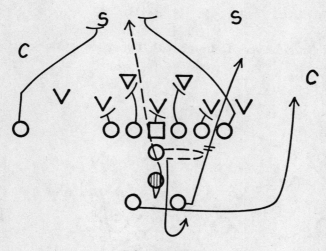

**Diagram 8-9**
**Outside Veer Counter**

Combination blocking is good to use with the Outside Veer Counter. Twenty-Five, Twenty-Three, Fifty-Three and Fifty-One blocking can be called and used. Diagrams 8-10, 8-11, 8-12, and 8-13 show the combination blocking.

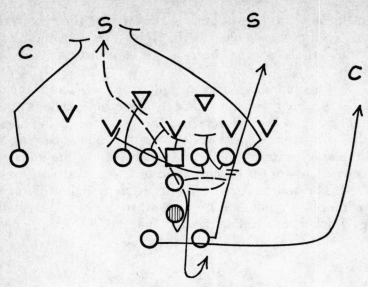

**Diagram 8-10**
**Outside Veer Counter with Twenty-Five Blocking**

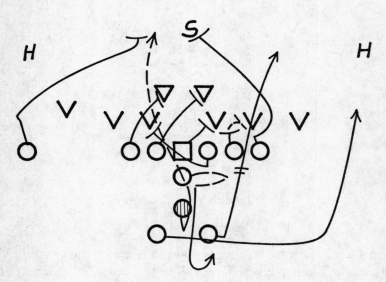

**Diagram 8-11**
**Outside Veer Counter with Twenty-Three Blocking**

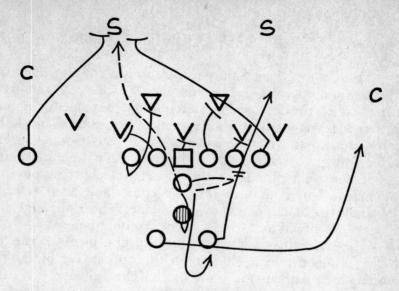

**Diagram 8-12**
**Outside Veer Counter with Fifty-Three Blocking**

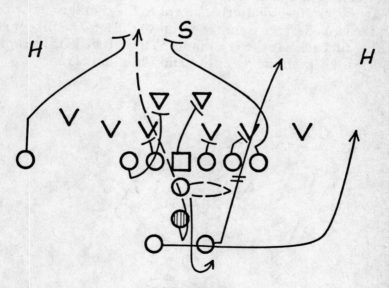

**Diagram 8-13**
**Outside Veer Counter with Fifty-One Blocking**

## OUTSIDE VEER COUNTER OPTION

The Outside Veer Counter Option is a counter play that attacks wide, opposite the original fake. It still has an internal fake to freeze the defense. The left end releases downfield hard for five to seven yards. Then he turns to the inside to block the first defensive pursuit that comes across the field. The left tackle, left guard, center and right guard all base block taking their defensive men to the right. The right tackle fires out into the man aligned on him for one count and then releases downfield to block in the running lane. The right end also releases downfield and blocks in the running lane.

The left halfback jab-steps to the right, pivots to the left and becomes the lead blocker on the option. He blocks the contain man with a side body block. The fullback fakes the Outside Veer Counter very hard trying to get tackled on the fake. The right halfback takes a jab step to the right, pivots left and runs an option path looking for the pitch from the quarterback. The quarterback steps to the right just as he does on the Outside Veer Counter, pivots to the left and fakes to the diving fullback. He then continues to the left making the option pitch or keep on the defensive end (Diagram 8-14).

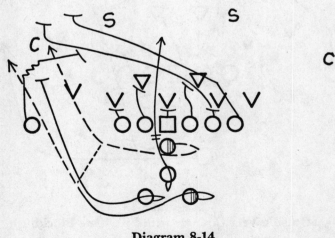

**Diagram 8-14**
**Outside Veer Counter Option**

## OUTSIDE VEER HOT PASS

The Hot Pass is effective from the Outside Veer fake. The left end runs a slant route. Although he is not the primary receiver, he may become the primary receiver if he is continually open. He tells the quarterback and the Outside Veer Hot Pass is called, with the quarterback looking for the left end first. All internal linemen block out aggressively, with the uncovered left guard or center dropping back to block on the back side. The right end fakes inside as if to block as he does on the Outside Veer running plays. Then he releases upfield looking for the pass. He takes a route to avoid linebackers getting into a line between him and the quarterback.

The right halfback fakes the Outside Veer dive very hard. The fullback will run the same course as he does on the Outside Veer option. He looks to receive the ball in the flat on a flare pattern after he turns upfield. The left halfback comes across to the right and stops to block the first defensive man to show outside the right tackle's block. A strong point to make is that the left halfback must always be alert to prevent a runback if there should be an interception. He is in the best position to help the quarterback to tackle an interceptor.

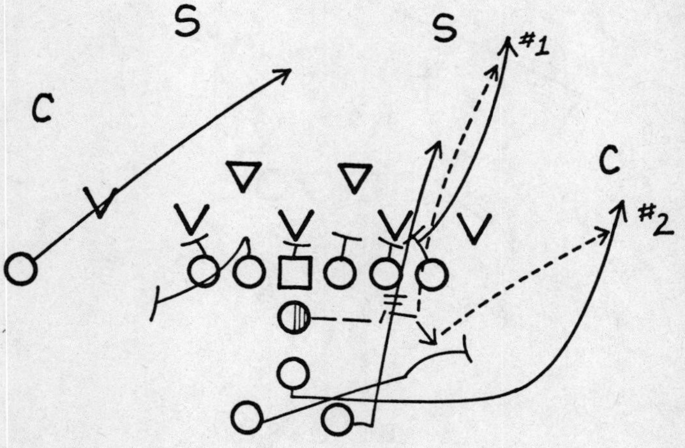

**Diagram 8-15**
**Outside Veer Hot Pass**

The quarterback steps out down the line, faking the Outside Veer dive and then raises up to look for the right end as a first choice. He should deliver the ball hard and chest high. If the right end is not open, the quarterback steps back one step and looks to deliver the ball to the fullback on a flare route as a second choice (Diagram 8-15).

## OUTSIDE VEER COUNTER PASS

The cross pass pattern is used for the Outside Veer Counter Pass. The left end runs a cross pattern eleven to 14 yards deep. He will cut in front of the right end who runs a streak route. The right end runs through the safety to take him deep. The right halfback fakes the Outside Veer dive and continues on to run an out pattern about eight yards deep. The fullback fakes the Outside Veer counter. The left halfback comes across to the right to block the defensive end. All the internal linemen have regular pass blocking responsibilities (Diagram 8-16).

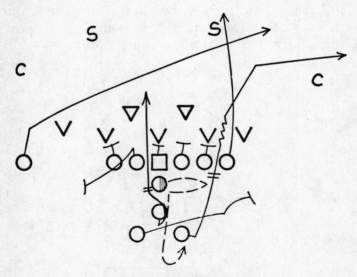

**Diagram 8-16**
**Outside Veer Counter Pass**

# CHAPTER 9

## Coaching the Wishbone Sprint Out Series

The Sprint Out Series is good to use in any T-formation system. It fits in the Wishbone very well and helps give the Multiple Wishbone versatility. The Sprint Out Series has these strong points from the Wishbone:

1. A complete series of plays can be run from the sprint out action.
2. The Sprint Out Series gives the talented quarterback the opportunity to run and pass more.
3. There is the option of running on all passes.
4. It gives the quarterback a chance to pass from a series in which he can focus all his attention on reading the defensive secondary.
5. The Sprint Out Series can be run from the basic Wishbone alignment as well as from various Broken Bone alignments.

The type and number of sprint out plays can vary from year to year. Team talents will help to determine this.

### ROUTES

The left halfback has the greatest variety of routes to run. He is the primary receiver on the greatest number of passes.

**145**

The passing routes of the primary receivers and names are in Diagram 9-1.

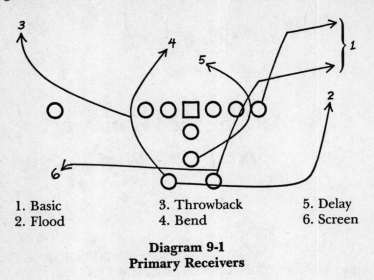

| 1. Basic | 3. Throwback | 5. Delay |
| 2. Flood | 4. Bend | 6. Screen |

**Diagram 9-1**
**Primary Receivers**

## PASS PROTECTION

The pass protection blocking for the Sprint Out Series is the same as the blocking used for the basic passing attack. All blocking is the aggressive fire-out type to make contact and maintain contact with the defensive man. All covered linemen execute the aggressive fire-out block. The uncovered linemen will start a fire-out block and then pull up to look for a stunt or blitz. The uncovered left guard or center will drop back to block on the back side (Diagrams 9-2 and 9-3).

The fullback has a critical block in the Sprint Out Series. He sprints to the onside to block the defensive end. He goes to a point one to one-and-one-half yards in front of where the defensive end aligned. The fullback executes a low, left shoulder block, driving his head past the defensive end's knee. If the defensive end starts to slip off the low shoulder block, the fullback goes down on all fours (hands and feet all on the ground) and scrambles on into the defensive end to keep his legs tied up. This also helps to keep the defensive end's hands down so the quarterback can see his receivers better (Diagram 9-4).

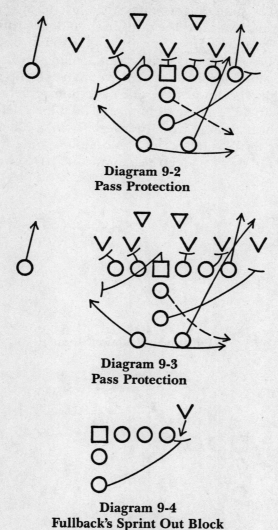

**Diagram 9-2**
**Pass Protection**

**Diagram 9-3**
**Pass Protection**

**Diagram 9-4**
**Fullback's Sprint Out Block**

## BASIC PASS

The left end executes either a streak route through the safety area or a deep drag route seven to nine yards deep. All the internal linemen execute their aggressive fire-out pass blocking techniques. The right end runs a flag route, reading the defensive man aligned in the deep outside zone. He releases, running toward the outside shoulder of this defensive secondary man. The right end drives the defensive secondary man back and outside as far as he can, looking for the pass over his outside shoulder. If the defensive man rolls up and comes past the right end toward the line of scrimmage, the right end cuts out toward the sidelines immediately. This sideline cut will get the right end away from the safety who is rolling to cover him. In the Sprint Out Series this optional route by the right end is refered to as a "deep reaction route" (Diagram 9-5).

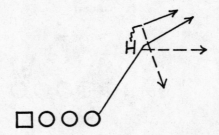

**Diagram 9-5**
**Right End's Reaction Route**

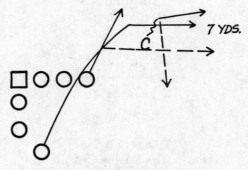

**Diagram 9-6**
**Right Halfback's Reaction Route**

The right halfback releases to run a flat route. He reads the contain man to tell him the depth that he will run. The right halfback goes to a depth of seven yards if the contain man will go that deep with him. He will cut to the sidelines immediately if the contain man passes by him to rush the passer. In the Sprint Out Series this optional route by the right halfback is referred to as a "short reaction route" (Diagram 9-6).

The fullback executes a low shoulder block on the defensive end. The left halfback comes across to the right and support blocks on the defensive end outside the fullback. The quarterback sprints to the right at a 45-degree angle. He open-steps with his right foot first and crosses over with his left foot on his second step to get depth and width. He moves the football into passing position as quickly as possible after receiving the snap. This position is chest-high, holding the ball with both hands, with the passing hand in position on the ball to throw it. The quarterback levels off at about five yards deep, getting outside to execute the pass-run option. The right end, right halfback and quarterback want to get a three-on-two situation against the defender in the deep outside third and the contain man. The quarterback reads the defense and looks for the right end first, the right halfback second and the left end third. If no receiver is open or if there is a good running lane open, the quarterback calls "block" and runs the football. The receivers will then peel back to block for him (Diagram 9-7).

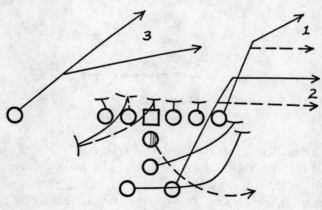

**Diagram 9-7**
**Basic Sprint Out Pass**

## FLOOD PASS

The area on one side of the field will have three receivers flooded into it. There are one major and two minor assignment changes between the Flood and Basic Sprint Out passes. The major assignment change is that the left halfback will run a flare route to the right. In the minor assignment changes, the right halfback will run a flat route at a depth of seven yards. The fullback must now block the defensive end alone. All other player assignments remain the same as in the Basic Sprint Out Pass. The quarterback reads the defense, looking to pass to the right end first, the right halfback second and the left halfback third. The left halfback will be open quite often on a short pass into the flat. The other receivers will peel back and block for him. If no receiver is open, the quarterback calls "block" and runs the football (Diagram 9-8).

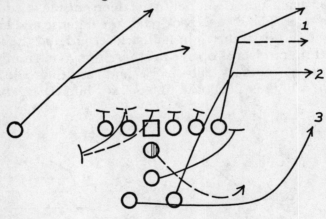

**Diagram 9-8**
**Flood Sprint Out Pass**

A flood variation run into the split end side is a good pass to get the right halfback open deep. The only changes involve the right end and the right halfback. The right end executes a curl route at ten to 12 yards deep. The right halfback runs an out-and-up route, trying to get as deep as possible to the outside. Aligning in a slot formation in the Broken Bone helps him to get out quicker. The quarterback now looks for the right

halfback first, the right end second and the left halfback third
(Diagram 9-9).

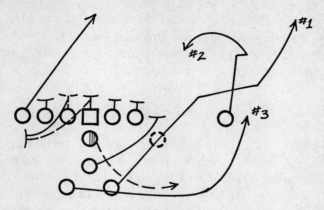

**Diagram 9-9**
**Flood Sprint Out Pass Variation**

## THROWBACK PASS

The primary receiver is the left halfback who runs an out-
and-up route to the left side. The left end runs a curl route ten
to 12 yards deep. The routes for the Throwback Pass are similar

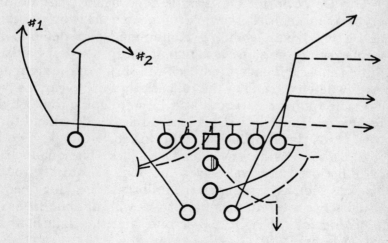

**Diagram 9-10**
**Throwback Sprint Out Pass**

to those for the Flood Variation except that the sprint flow fake
is opposite. All internal assignments are the same as those on
the Basic Sprint Out pass. The right end runs a deep reaction
route. The right halfback has the option of running a short
reaction route or helping the fullback block the defensive end.
The quarterback should drop three or four yards deeper to
make the longer crossfield throw (Diagram 9-10).

## BEND PASS

The Bend In route by the left halfback and a flag route by
the left end are the only changes in the Bend Pass from the
Basic Pass. The left halfback finds the first daylight to the left of
the left tackle to run through and bends in slightly to the right
as he goes downfield. The left end runs a flag route to take the
defensive man deep and to the outside. The quarterback will
pull up to throw a little quicker for he wants to deliver the ball
to the left halfback as soon as he clears the linebackers. This is a
good pass to use against a secondary that flows fast to stop the
Basic Sprint Out pass (Diagram 9-11).

## DELAY PASS

The Delay Sprint Out Pass is good against fast flowing
linebackers or linebackers who drop deep quickly on passes. It
is also a good pass against a man-to-man pass defense. All
players execute the same assignment except the left halfback
and the fullback. The left halfback will sprint to the right and
block the defensive end as the fullback slips off to run his pass
route. The fullback starts out as if he were going to block the
defensive end, and then slips off and releases downfield three
to five yards, bending back to the inside. He looks for the
football as soon as he leaves his fake block. The quarterback
should be prepared to deliver the football quickly to the
fullback as soon as he sees that the fullback is breaking open. If
the fullback is covered, the quarterback will continue sprinting
out looking for the right end second, and the right halfback
third (Diagram 9-12).

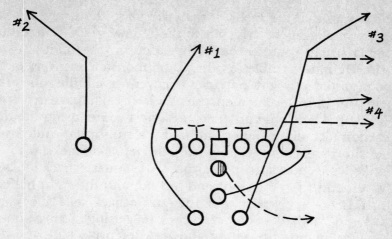

**Diagram 9-11**
**Bend Sprint Out Pass**

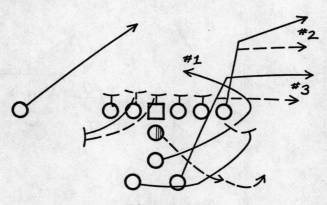

**Diagram 9-12**
**Delay Sprint Out Pass**

## SPECIAL PASS

This is a special pass that is used against a monster or invert type of secondary defense. The pass is executed from a Broken Bone Pro formation. The left halfback aligns ten to 12 yards outside the left end. This is done to spread the defense and insure that the monster man will go to the strength of the offensive alignment, which is to the offense's left. The left end runs a streak route through the safety or the middle of the field. He must be able to outrun the monster or invert man if the monster or invert man tries to cover the middle zone of the field. All internal linemen uses their regular pass protection blocking. The right end executes a post route, using the deep reaction technique. The right halfback runs a flat route using, the short reaction technique. The left halfback, who has flanked, executes a deep flag route. The quarterback looks for the left end first, the right end second, and the right halfback third. If no receiver is open, the quarterback yells "block" and runs the football. The receivers are getting a three-on-two situation against the safety and left defensive halfback (Diagram 9-13).

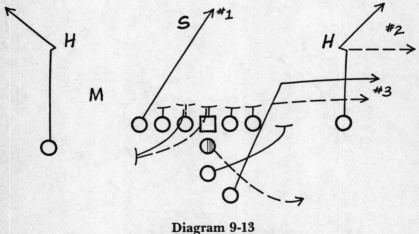

**Diagram 9-13**
**Special Sprint Out Pass**

## SIDE SCREEN PASS

The pressure put on the defense to the sprint side will make the side screen opposite the flow very effective. The left end runs a streak route through the safety and then peels back to the left to block. The left tackle, left guard and center fire out aggressively for two counts. They execute screen blocking by appearing to be beaten by their opponents. Then the left tackle pulls to the left for four yards and pivots back to block to the inside. The left guard pulls to the left and blocks to the outside. His block will be three yards outside the left tackle. The center's path will be between the left tackle's and left guard's blocks. If no defensive man is in the area to block, the left tackle and left guard lead on downfield to block. The right guard and right tackle execute aggressive fire-out blocks straight ahead. The right end runs a flag route and sprints back to the left to block.

The fullback executes his normal sprint out block on the defensive end. The left halfback sprints to the right, sets up to block for three counts, and then flares to the right as an outlet receiver if the primary receiver, the right halfback, is not open. The right halfback takes one step toward the line of scrimmage and then sprints to the left to set up for the screen pass from the quarterback. He sets up four yards outside where the left end aligns in tight alignment. This will put him about one yard

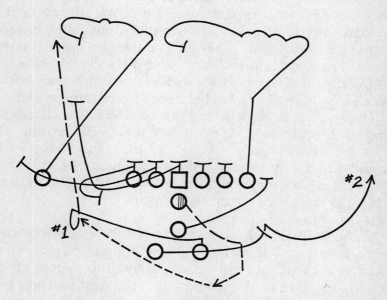

**Diagram 9-14**
**Sprint Out Side Screen Pass**

outside and back of the left tackle's block and inside the left guard's block.

The quarterback sprints out to the right just as he would on the Basic Sprint Out pass. Then he drops quickly to get more depth to pass to the right halfback. The added depth is to insure that the pass is forward and not backward. Then if the pass is dropped, it is only an incomplete pass and not a backward pass that might be recovered or advanced by the defensive team. Upon receiving the football, the right halfback will call "block" and run into the running lane created by the three pulling linemen. If the right halfback is covered, the quarterback looks for the left halfback who has flared to the right (Diagram 9-14).

## MIDDLE SCREEN PASS

The Sprint Out Middle Screen Pass is very effective against the hard middle rush and shooting linebackers. The left end runs his regular route through the safety and then looks to block the first man to come into this area. All the internal linemen will execute their regular sprint out pass protection blocking for two counts. They act as if they are beaten on their blocks. Then they release downfield to block the first opponent to appear in their area. The left guard or center who drops to block to the left will also hold his block for two counts and then peel to the right to block behind the fullback who is the primary receiver for the pass. Many times there will be one alert defender who will turn quickly and catch the receiver from behind as he may have to slow up momentarily to pick his running lane among the blockers ahead of him. The right end and right halfback execute Basic Sprint Out pass routes and then sprint to the left to block.

The left halfback blocks the defensive end to the right. The quarterback will sprint to the right just as he does on the Basic Sprint Out pass, and then quickly drop to get depth to pass to the fullback, who has started to the right for three steps and then goes to the left and sets up behind the center right guard gap to receive the pass. He stays low to hide himself from the defense. He calls "block" upon receiving the ball and runs to daylight behind the internal linemen's blocking (Diagram 9-15).

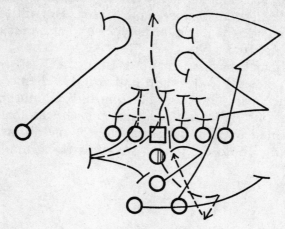

**Diagram 9-15**
**Sprint Out Middle Screen Pass**

## SPRINT OUT DRAW

The draw play must be included in the Sprint Out Series since many good gainers will result from the proper execution of this play. The left end executes his normal route through the safety area and then looks to the left to block. All the internal linemen fire aggressively to block. Then they maintain contact and work their defensive opponents to the outside away from the left guard area where the football is going to be run. The left guard has the option of taking his man either way that he wants to go. The right end executes his normal flag route and then sprints to the left to block.

The fullback blocks the defensive end just as he does on the Basic Sprint Out pass. The left halfback shows pass protection blocking to the left and then leads through the left guard area to block a linebacker or the first opponent to show. The right halfback takes one step to the right and shows pass protection blocking, makes a pocket to receive the football by dropping the right hand and lower arm and raising the left arm and hand, and then receives the football from the quarterback as he comes by. After receiving the football, the right halfback runs for daylight in the left guard area. He will look to cut inside or outside the left guard's block and also take advantage of the left halfback's block.

The quarterback sprints out as on the Basic Sprint Out pass and hands off to the right halfback. He then continues to fake a Basic Sprint Out pass. The quarterback must come close by the waiting right halfback and put the football into the pocket formed by him, by taking the football in his left hand and lowering it into the pocket smoothly (Diagram 9-16).

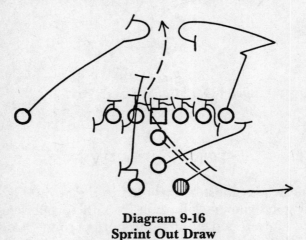

**Diagram 9-16**
**Sprint Out Draw**

## SPRINT OUT SWEEP

This is a predetermined sweep with the quarterback running the football. It blends in very well with the various sprint out passes and gives the running quarterback an excellent play and series from which to run the football. The Sprint Out Sweep must look like a pass as much as possible. The left end sprints through the safety on a streak route and then blocks. All the internal linemen fire out aggressively, trying to make their blocks resemble those used on the sprint out passes, and work their opponents to the left. The right end and right halfback both release and execute their routes just as in a Basic Sprint Out Pass. Then they peel to the left to block. This will form a running lane for the quarterback. The fullback and left halfback both block the defensive end, taking him in so the quarterback can get outside of him quickly. The quarterback sprints out just as he does on a pass, shows pass-faking the football, and cuts upfield taking advantage of his blocking (Diagram 9-17).

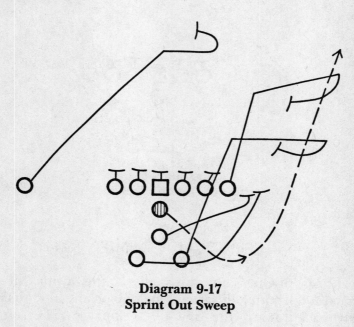

**Diagram 9-17**
**Sprint Out Sweep**

## SPRINT OUT OFF TACKLE

This is a power type of play that fits well into the sprint out sequence of plays. The left end sprints through the safety and blocks the first man to show. All the internal linemen fire out and pass block aggressively. The right end blocks the first defensive man to his inside. The fullback and right halfback block out on the defensive end. The left halfback leads through the six or off-tackle hole and blocks the first opponent to show. The close alignment of the halfbacks in the Wishbone allows the left halfback time to get ahead of the quarterback to block.

The quarterback sprints to the right, showing pass. He will quickly cut upfield when he reaches the six-hole area. He cuts between the double-team blocks of the right tackle and end and the right halfback and fullback. He also follows the left halfback and cuts off of his block (Diagram 9-18).

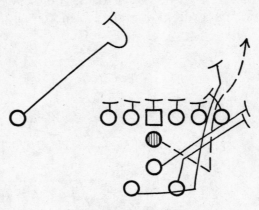

**Diagram 9-18**
**Sprint Out Off Tackle**

## SPRINT OUT COUNTER

The Sprint Out Counter is similar to the Sprint Out Draw but is executed with a different type of blocking and hits more quickly back toward the line of scrimmage. The left end releases downfield just as he does on the Basic Sprint Out pass and then looks to his left to block the first defender to show in the area. The internal linemen will execute Twenty-Three or Twenty-Five combination blocking. The left tackle will block to the inside and will have a coaching point made to block the linebacker against a split defense. The left guard will block the first defender to his inside. The center blocks the man on him or to the offside. The right guard pulls to the left and blocks the first man outside the left guard's alignment. The right tackle will check-block in the pulling right guard's area. The right end releases as he does on a Basic Sprint Out pass for six steps and then sprints to the left to block in the running lane.

The fullback blocks to the right picking up the first opponent to show outside the right tackle's block. The left halfback sprints to the right to block. The right halfback takes one step up and to the right, makes a pocket for receiving the football and cuts for the center's left foot. He receives the handoff from the quarterback cutting up between the right guard's trap block and the seal blocks of the left tackle and left guard. The quarterback sprints out, handing off to the right halfback as he comes by, and then continues his sprint out fake (Diagram 9-19).

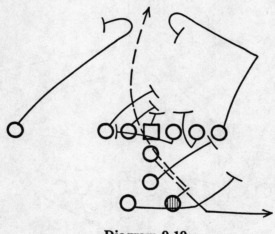

**Diagram 9-19**
**Sprint Out Counter**

## SPRINT OUT REVERSE

This is a trick type of play that blends into the Sprint Out Series very well. It can be included very easily since the blocking for the linemen is the same as that used for the Sprint Out Side Screen pass. This is regular screen blocking for the left tackle, left guard and center. Base blocking is used by the right guard and right tackle. The left end and right end execute their regular routes and peel back to block (see Diagram 9-14 for these assignments). The fullback also has the same assignment to block the defensive end. Only the halfbacks and quarterback execute differently. The right halfback runs a regular flat route and then sprints to the left to block. The left halfback comes across to the right and sets up to block two steps outside the right halfback's alignment. He is watching the quarterback out of the corner of his eye and will pivot to the right and start to the left to receive the handoff when the quarterback is three steps from him. After receiving the handoff, the left halfback sprints wide to the left, picking up the screen blocking path formed by the left tackle, left guard and center. The quarterback sprints out, showing pass, and hands off with the right hand to the left halfback who is sprinting to the left (Diagram 9-20).

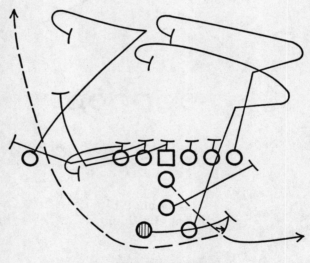

**Diagram 9-20**
**Sprint Out Reverse**

# CHAPTER *10*

# *Coaching the Flip-Flop Wishbone*

The Flip-Flop principle simplifies offensive football. Only one-half as many offensive assignments have to be learned. Instead of only the ends flip-flopping, the entire line and halfbacks flip-flop from the huddle (Diagrams 10-1 and 10-2).

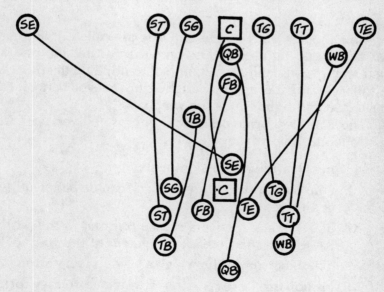

**Diagram 10-1**
**Huddle and Flip-Flop to the Right**

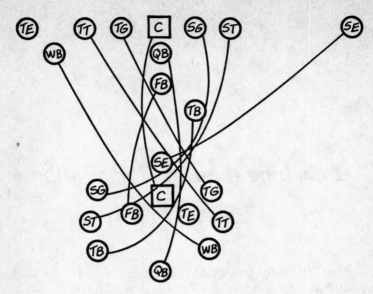

**Diagram 10-2**
**Huddle and Flip-Flop to the Left**

The linemen on the tight end side are called tight guard, tight tackle and tight end. The linemen on the split end are called split guard, split tackle and split end. The deep back is the tailback and the up back aligned in the slot between the tight tackle and tight end is the wingback.

The Flip-Flop principle can be intergrated very well with the Wishbone. The advantages are:

1. Less learning on assignments.
2. One outstanding running back can be better utilized at tailback.
3. Three quick receivers can be released in the passing game with the slotback placement of the wingback.
4. The blocking to the wingback side is very strong.
5. Motion can be used with the wingback to vary formations (Diagram 10-3).

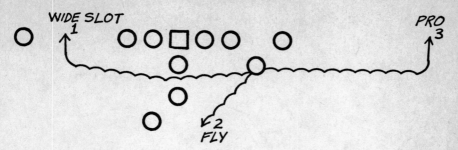

**Diagram 10-3**
**Motion by the Wingback in the Flip-Flop Wishbone**

All regular Wishbone plays, plus any special plays to fit a team's abilities, can be run from the Flip-Flop Wishbone. Diagrams 10-4 through 10-28 show a complete set of plays for the Flip-Flop Wishbone. No explanations are given since all assignments remain the same for the Flip-Flop Wishbone as they do for the regular Wishbone plays, which are fully explained in other chapters.

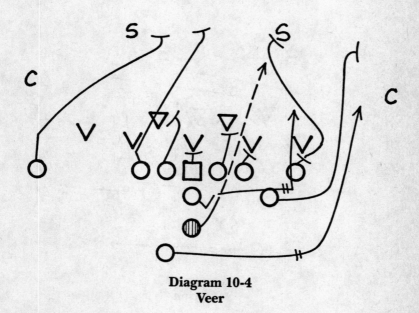

**Diagram 10-4**
**Veer**

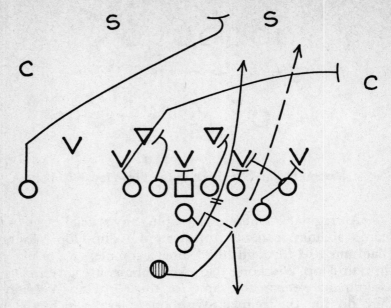

**Diagram 10-5**
**Belly**

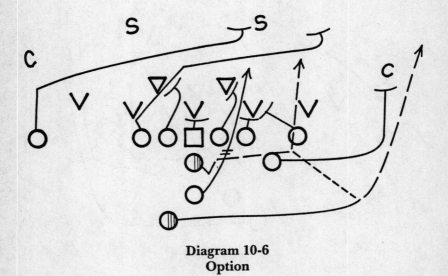

**Diagram 10-6**
**Option**

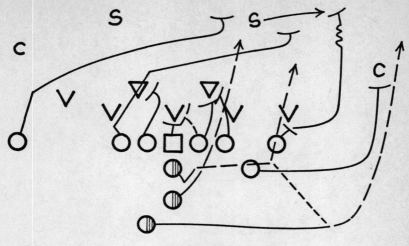

**Diagram 10-7**
**Triple Option**

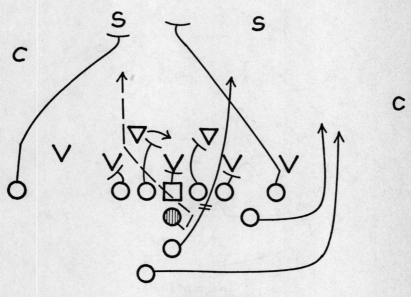

**Diagram 10-8**
**Quarterback Counter**

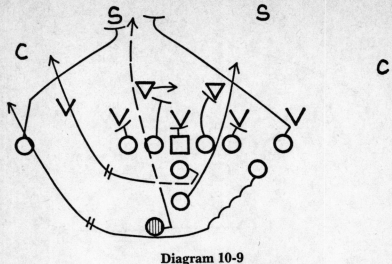

**Diagram 10-9**
**Counter Dive**

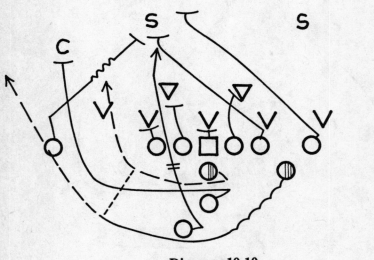

**Diagram 10-10**
**Counter Option**

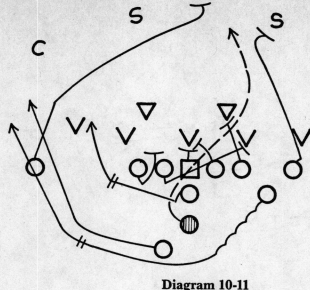

**Diagram 10-11**
**Fullback Trap**

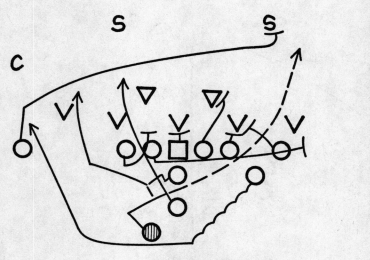

**Diagram 10-12**
**Crossbuck**

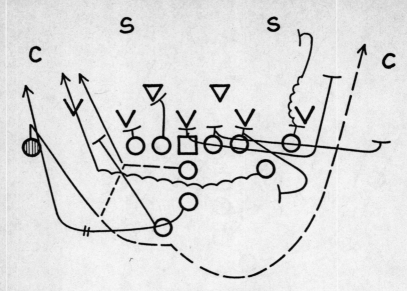

**Diagram 10-13**
**Wide Reverse**

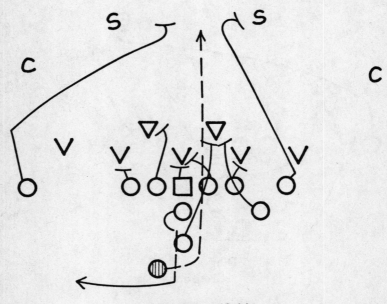

**Diagram 10-14**
**Inside Power**

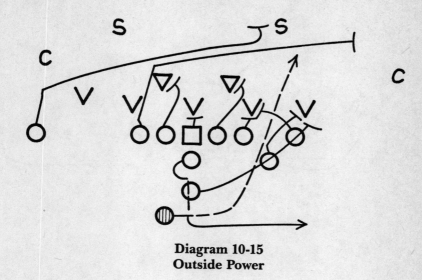

**Diagram 10-15**
**Outside Power**

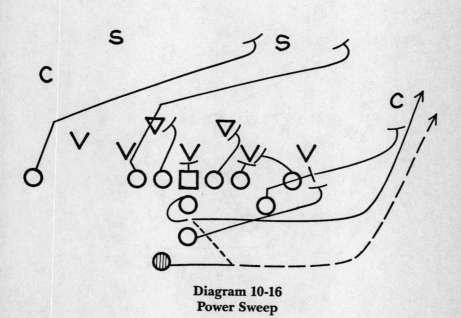

**Diagram 10-16**
**Power Sweep**

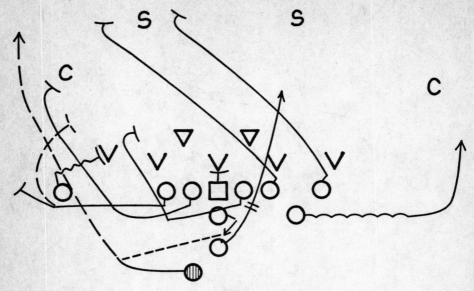

**Diagram 10-17**
**Quick Pitch**

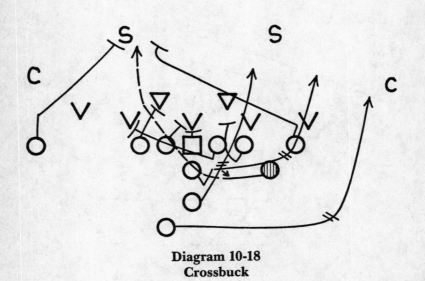

**Diagram 10-18**
**Crossbuck**

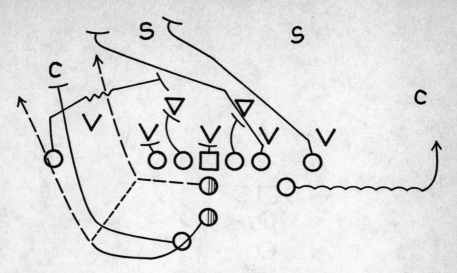

**Diagram 10-19**
**Speed Option**

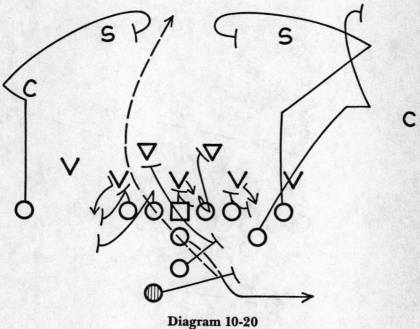

**Diagram 10-20**
**Draw**

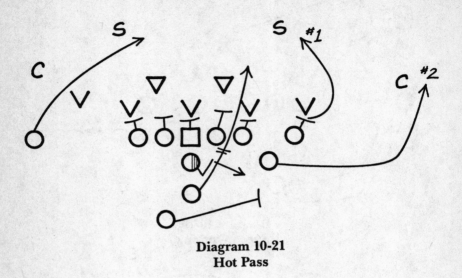

**Diagram 10-21**
**Hot Pass**

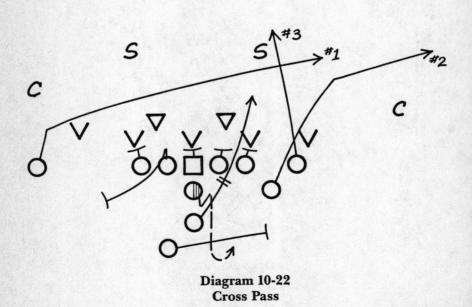

**Diagram 10-22**
**Cross Pass**

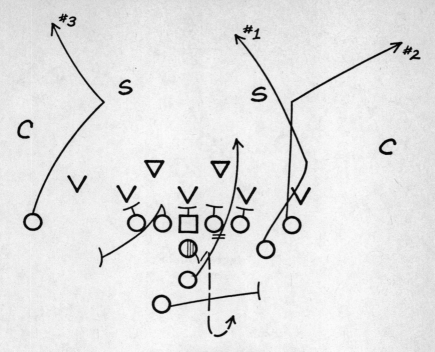

**Diagram 10-23**
**Divide Pass**

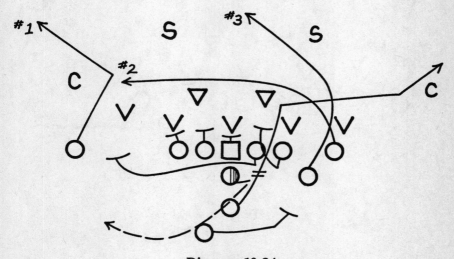

**Diagram 10-24**
**Bootleg Pass**

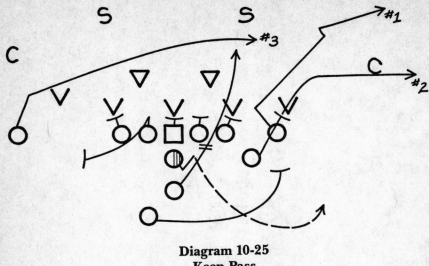

**Diagram 10-25**
**Keep Pass**

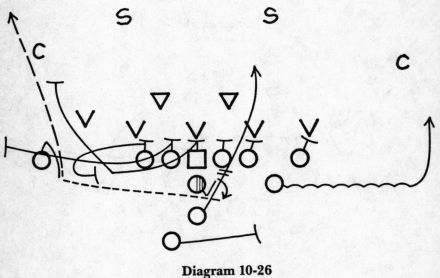

**Diagram 10-26**
**Quick Screen**

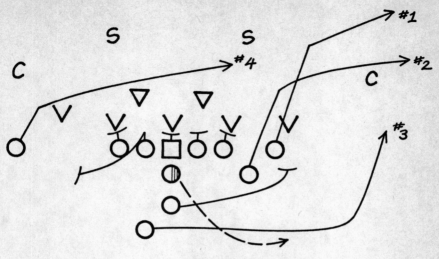

**Diagram 10-27**
**Flood Sprint Out Pass**

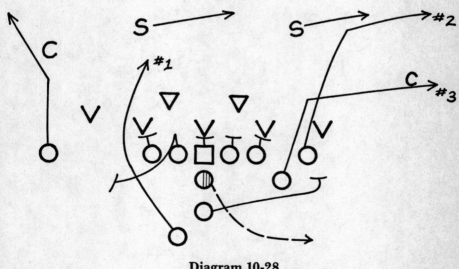

**Diagram 10-28**
**Bend Sprint Out Pass**

# CHAPTER *11*

## *Special Wishbone Plays*

Some Wishbone plays are of a special type. These are included and used in special situations and special games. They are also used by teams with special talents at certain positions.

## SELECTION AND USE

Special plays should be selected and used wisely. There are several factors that will determine their selection and use. They are:

1. Special plays should be used sparingly.
2. Special plays should be installed sparingly.
3. Have a purpose for each special play.
4. Do not add special plays just for the sake of having new plays.
5. Add plays to:
   A. Take advantage of the opponent's
      (1). Defensive alignment
      (2). Defensive secondary coverage
      (3). Defensive stunts
      (4). Defensive assignments
      (5). Secondary rotation
      (6). Defensive tendencies. (Scouting reports and film study will determine the above six things.)

  B. Complement your other most successful plays.

  C. Combat staleness on the part of the offense.

  D. To gain a psychological advantage.

  E. To confuse or fool the defense.

 6. Add special plays according to the ability of the team's personnel.

The special plays are divided into five classifications. They are internal plays that attack from off tackle to the inside, wide plays that go outside end, draws that fake a pass and then develop into a run, screens that have different receivers, and special passes.

## INTERNAL

Internal plays attack from the off-tackle area to the inside, three are included as special plays. They are supplementary to other Wishbone plays.

The *slant play* is a way to run the fullback off tackle. It is also a counter flow play that attacks wider than the counter dive and inside the counter option. Some defenses will defend against only the counter dive and counter option when they see that the counter flow is coming. If the defense does this, the off-tackle area is open for the slant play.

The left end releases downfield and executes a cross-body block in the running lane. The left tackle blocks the man on him for two counts and then releases downfield to block in the running lane. The left guard and center base block their defensive men to the left. The right guard will base block to the left or execute a Twenty-Six block by pulling and blocking the defensive end out. The right tackle base blocks to the left or pulls and blocks the defensive end if a Forty-Six block is called. The right end base blocks to the inside.

The right halfback fakes the counter dive very hard, trying to freeze the internal defensive men. The left halfback fakes the counter option. The quarterback fakes the counter dive to the right halfback and continues down the line as he does in the counter option. After two steps, the quarterback meshes with the slanting fullback and hands the ball to him. Then the quarterback fakes the counter option pitch to the left halfback. The fullback starts as if he is going wide to block on the counter option. Then he slants into the off-tackle area over the six hole or right end. He receives the ball from the quarterback and cuts upfield between the right end and the combination block of either the right guard (26 block) or right tackle (46 block) (Diagram 11-1).

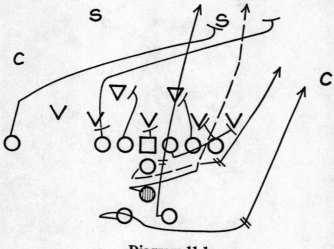

**Diagram 11-1**
**Slant with 26 Blocking**

The *lead play* is another play from counter flow action. The lead play lets the offense run off tackle with a double-team block or a good angle block. The left end and the left tackle have the same assignments as they do on the slant play; release and block downfield in the running lane. All other linemen base block to the left. The right halfback fakes a counter dive very hard to freeze the internal defense. The fullback executes an Eight-Six block on the defensive end. The quarterback fakes a counter dive to the right halfback and comes back away from the line of scrimmage slightly as he takes another step to hand off to the left halfback. Then the quarterback fakes on to the outside. The left halfback takes a jab step to the left and starts a counter option route to the right. He continues this route until he clears the right halfback's original alignment. Then he cuts up into the off-tackle hole over the inside foot of the right end. He receives the ball from the quarterback and runs between the base block of the right end and the inside-out block of the fullback (Diagram 11-2).

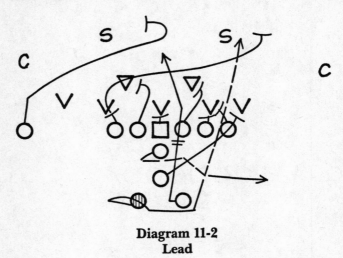

**Diagram 11-2**
**Lead**

The lead play can have blocking variations. Twenty-Six or Forty-Six blocking would be the most commonly used combination blocking variations. If either of these types of blocking variations is used, the fullback may lead through the hole to block or fake a Veer play to the left.

The *crisscross play* is a special play to complement the crossbuck and should be considered for use after the crossbuck is successful and the defense is looking for the crossbuck.

The crisscross uses combination blocking. All the linemen base block to the left except the left end, who blocks downfield in the running lane, and the right guard or right tackle who will block out on the defensive end. Twenty-Six or Forty-Six blocking is used. The fullback fakes the Veer play very hard to freeze the defense. The right halfback fakes the crossbuck to freeze the defense also. The left halfback takes a jab step to the left for timing purposes and then takes an angle course over the right end's inside leg. He receives the football from the quarterback and runs upfield between the block of the right end and the combination blocker, who is either the right guard or right tackle. The quarterback fakes the Veer to the fullback, the crossbuck to the right halfback and then takes a step back and hands off to the left halfback. Then the quarterback drops quickly and fakes a pass (Diagram 11-3).

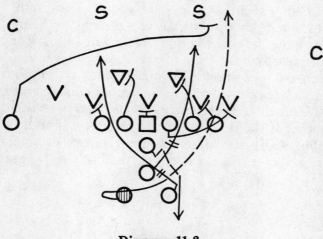

**Diagram 11-3**
**Crisscross with 26 Blocking**

A good variation of the crisscross is to use 326 blocking. This combination blocking variation has both guards pulling. The right guard blocks out on the defensive end and the left guard pulls through the six hole and blocks upfield.

## WIDE

Wide special plays are option variations and reverse variations. The *speed option* is a very good special play when the fullback has the speed to run outside. It is a good option to run from the Broken Bone sets, especially the Pro and Twin sets. It is a very good play to run into the split end side of the formation using the Pro set. Very few new assignments are required. Most assignments remain the same as in the regular option.

The left end and left tackle release downfield and execute side body blocks in the running lane. All the other internal linemen (left guard, center, right guard, and right tackle) base block to the left. The split end releases downfield and blocks the defensive man responsible for the outside deep third of the secondary. The flanked left halfback releases downfield to block or to execute some pass route. The right halfback executes a regular option play assignment by being the lead blocker on the defensive contain man. The fullback angles back on his first steps to the right to gain depth. This is in order to be in correct pitch position if the quarterback pitches to him. The quarterback sprints down the line under control and reads the defensive end. He keeps or pitches according to the defensive end's move. If the defensive end crashes on him, he pitches to the fullback. If the defensive end boxes or contains, the quarterback cuts upfield keeping the football (Diagram 11-4).

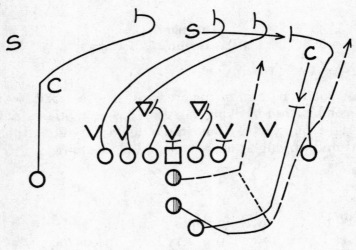

**Diagram 11-4**
**Speed Option**

Other special option plays are a *load option* from the regular Wishbone alignment. The only change from the regular option is that there is no fullback veer fake. The fullback sprints outside with the lead halfback and blocks downfield in the deep outside third of the secondary.

The *counter load option* is another special play with only one assignment change from the regular counter option. This involves the left halfback. He does not fake a counter dive, but leads outside to the left to block in the deep outside third of the secondary.

*Reverses* are the other type of wide special plays. One type of wide reverse, described in Chapter 6, uses the split end as the ball carrier. Screen blocking is used on all reverses. Reverses can be executed from various sets and by different players at different positions.

You must evaluate personnel and formations and pick out the best formation and the best player to run the reverse. The reverse can be executed from both option and draw fakes. When the option fake is executed, the right halfback from a regular position or flanked in the pro or twins formation will be the ball carrier. The right end may also be used to carry the ball on the reverse play.

The left end blocks downfield to the inside. The left tackle, left guard and center execute screen blocking. The right guard and right tackle base block. The right end will also base block if he is not the ball carrier. If he is going to be the ball carrier, he will block outside for one count, slip off and get depth quickly going to the left to receive the pitch from the quarterback. The left halfback fakes an option play to the right. The fullback fakes the veer play. The right halfback, from a regular position, goes to the right and then pivots back to the left to receive the pitch from the quarterback. If the right halfback is flanked in either the pro or twins set, he will immediately sprint back to the left to receive the pitch. The right halfback blocks just outside the right tackle if the right end is the ball carrier.

The quarterback fakes the veer to the fullback, continues on down the line two steps and pitches to the reverse ball carrier. He then cuts upfield as he does on the option. Timing is very important and has to be worked out on an experimental basis according to the speed of the ball carrier and the quickness of the quarterback. Diagram 11-5 shows the reverse from an option fake with the various ball carrier possibilities.

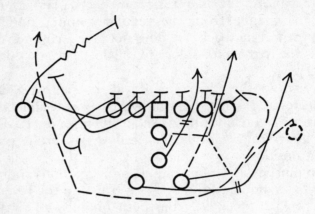

**Diagram 11-5**
**Option Reverse (Halfback or End Carrying Ball)**

The *fake draw reverse* will use either a flanked right half-back or the fullback to carry the football. The line execution is the same for the fake draw reverse as it is for the option reverse; screen blocking on the left side and base blocking on the right side. The fake draw reverse can best be executed from a pro or twins formation. The fullback will block to the right if the right halfback is the ball carrier or fake blocking, pivot back and start to the left and take a handoff from the quarterback and run wide to the left behind the screen blocks. The left halfback comes to the right, fakes a block and fakes the draw play into the one-hole area.

The right halfback executes a pass route if the fullback is the ball carrier. He sprints quickly to the left and receives a handoff from the quarterback if he is the ball carrier. The right end executes a pass route if he is in an open position and base blocks if he is tight. The quarterback fakes a sprint out pass, then fakes a draw to the left halfback. Then he hands off to either the fullback or right halfback to run the reverse. This is a handoff behind the quarterback and made with his right hand. He then continues to the right and gets depth while faking a pass. Diagram 11-6 shows the fake draw reverse.

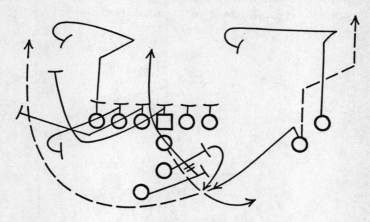

**Diagram 11-6**
**Fake Draw Reverse (Halfback or Fullback Carrying Ball)**

## DRAWS

There are two special draw plays; the *quarterback draw* and the *sprint draw*. These can be considered as the principal draw plays, instead of others, because of personnel or the opponent's defense.

The quarterback draw is a good draw for several reasons. It can be run from the regular Wishbone set or any Broken Bone formation. Since Wishbone quarterbacks have running ability, the quarterback draw gives the quarterback another opportunity to run the football. It is a simple draw to execute against any defense. Wide-out players, ends and any back in a broken set sprint downfield and execute a pass route and then sprint to a position to block in the running lane. All internal linemen pass-block, working their man to the outside. The fullback shows a block to the right and then quickly leads through to block on a linebacker. The halfbacks pass-block to their respective sides if they are in their regular alignment.

They execute a pass route and block downfield if they are in a broken set. The quarterback shows pass by dropping three steps, straight back quickly. He holds the ball high with both hands. The ball is in passing position so the defense can see it. He quickly drops the ball into running position and runs into the zero-hole area, following and cutting off the fullback's block (Diagram 11-7).

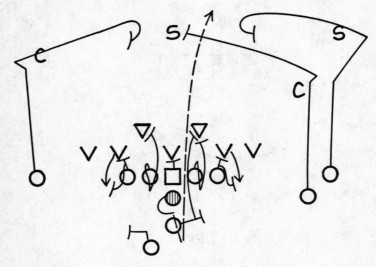

**Diagram 11-7**
**Quarterback Draw**

The sprint draw, hitting into the off-tackle area to the sprint fake side, is different from other draws that attack internally or away from the sprint pass fake. The regular Wishbone formation or broken sets may be used. The left end executes a pass route and then sprints to the right to block. All other linemen base block to the left. The fullback blocks out on the defensive end with an Eighty-Six (86) block. The left halfback blocks to the left if he is in regular position. He executes a pass route and blocks downfield if he aligns in a Broken Bone set. The right halfback jab-steps to the right and shows pass blocking. He makes a pocket and receives the ball from the quarterback. He then runs into the six-hole area. He will cut between the right end's block to the inside and the fullback's block outside. The quarterback sprints to the right as he does on sprint passes. He hands off to the right halfback and continues his pass fake to the right (Diagram 11-8).

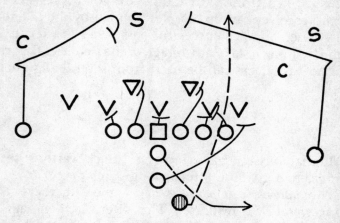

**Diagram 11-8**
**Sprint Draw from Strong Pro**

## SCREENS

Screens are a vital part of the Multiple Wishbone offense. They are used effectively to cut down on the pass rush and by

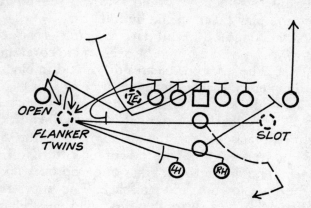

**Diagram 11-9**
**Different Screen Alignments and Positions**

the quarterback who is not a good long passer. Screens can be thrown from several play action fakes and to several different receivers. The *sprint out action screen* is very good since a lot of Multiple Wishbone passing is done from the sprint out series. Screens thrown from a draw fake are good also. The type of fake and receiver can be best determined by the talents of the offensive personnel, a successful pass series to execute it from and the best way to take advantage of the defense. Diagram 11-9 shows how receivers can be used from several alignments and positions.

## PASSES

Special passes can effectively attack various secondary coverages and give the offense long gains.

The *automatic throwout pass* is good if there is single coverage against a twins set. This often happens against the Wishbone because defenses are so intent on stopping the running game. This is especially true if the defense uses a three-deep secondary. The throwout pass can be an automatic and executed whenever there is single coverage by the defense on a twins set. One way to execute the throwout pass is having only the receiver (the right halfback) and the quarterback communicate a signal to one another to put the automatic into effect. Using this method would have all the other players executing the play called in the huddle.

The other method would have the quarterback check off to the throwout pass any time he sees single coverage against the twins set. The left end releases downfield to block. All the internal linemen fire out with aggressive base blocks. The right end releases and blocks the secondary man who is in single coverage. The fullback and the left halfback fake to the right. The right halfback turns to the inside, receives the quick pass from the quarterback and runs downfield cutting off the right end's block. The quarterback takes one step back and quickly throws the pass to the right halfback. The quarterback and right halfback must be aware that their alignment is such that a forward pass is thrown. The quarterback must be deeper than the right halfback so the pass is forward and not backward in case the pass is incomplete. If the pass is made backward and is incomplete it is a lateral and the defense can recover it. Diagram 11-10 shows the throwout pass.

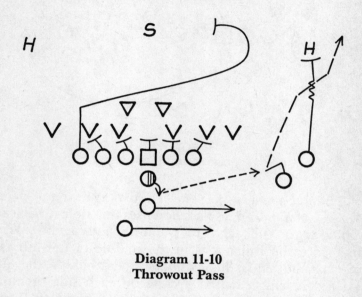

**Diagram 11-10**
**Throwout Pass**

A *maximum flood pass* (four receivers to one side of the defense) is a good special pass using the twins set. The defense is outnumbered and the quarterback has four receivers in his vision that he can throw to. The left end blocks to the back side. All the internal linemen base block except the right guard who pulls to block the defensive end. The right end runs a curl route ten to twelve yards deep. The right halfback runs an out-and-up route deep. The fullback goes as if to block as he does on a sprint out pass, makes contact for one count and then runs a deep flat route seven to nine yards deep. The left halfback sprints to the right, fakes a block, and flares into the shallow right flat. The quarterback sprints out and looks to pass to the right halfback, right end, fullback or left halfback in that order (Diagram 11-11).

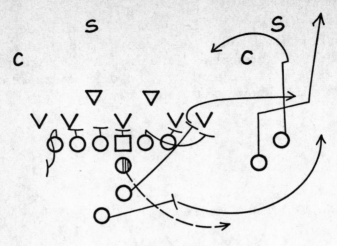

**Diagram 11-11**
**Maximum Flood Pass**

The *gut pass* can be very effective against two-deep pass defenses or man-to-man pass defenses that do not have anyone assigned to the fullback. This often happens against Wishbone teams since the fullback is in the middle of the offense and somewhat hidden by his close alignment behind the quarterback and having a halfback close on each side of him. The defense does not look for him to be a receiver. The ends execute flag routes. The right end can flex out some to spread the secondary. All internal linemen base block working their man to the outside. Both halfbacks take one step up and block against the outside rush. The fullback goes through the three-hole area and runs a bend route into the middle. He tries to get as deep and into the middle of the defense as quick as possible. The receivers (both ends and fullback) work to get a three-on-two situation deep against the defensive secondary. The quarterback pivots to the right to avoid the fullback, drops quickly about six to seven yards deep and looks to pass to the fullback in the middle of the defensive secondary. If the fullback is covered, he reads the defense and looks to see if one of the ends is open (Diagram 11-12).

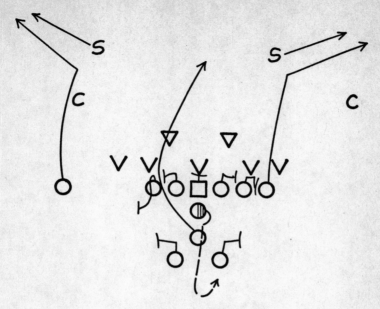

**Diagram 11-12**
**Gut Pass**

# CHAPTER 12

# *Installing and Using Wishbone Variations*

There will be more Wishbone variations in the offense as its use increases. These variations will evolve because smart defensive coaches will devise new defensive schemes against the basic alignment and basic plays. Individual defensive players will perform better against the basic Wishbone as they play against it more often and become familiar with its execution. This will cause Wishbone coaches to devise and add Wishbone variations. These variations will be in the form of:

1. Multiple formations by breaking the basic Wishbone set.
2. Men in motion.
3. Shifting into and out of the basic Wishbone.
4. Unbalancing.
5. Spreads.

Wishbone variations will vary according to several factors. They are:

1. The coach's philosophy about offense.
2. The players' abilities and talents.
3. Depth. A two-platoon team can master more offense.

4. The strength of the opposition.

5. The type of defense to be faced.

6. The game plan that is to be executed.

7. The game situation (score, time, weather and field conditions).

## FORMATIONS

The Wishbone is easy to adapt to multiple formations. It has been criticized as a poor "catch-up" offense. The use of multiple formations will eliminate this criticism. Formations are easy to learn. For this reason it is an advantage to the offense to have several formations to make the defense adjust, but little offensive time is used to learn formations. Most offensive plays can be run from several formations with little or no offensive adjustment.

Formations are given word descriptions instead of numbers. The descriptive word describes the formation. The descriptive word makes it easier for players to remember and there are no formations called by numbers that might be confused with play numbers or numbers called in combination blocking.

The pro, twins and twins open are all good broken bone sets. Other formations are the double tight, double open, wing, flanker, wide slot, short slot and strong sets.

The pro set is used to spread the defense both ways. The only change from the basic Wishbone formation is that the right halfback goes to the right twelve yards or no closer than seven yards of the sideline. He aligns one yard off the line of scrimmage. (Diagram 12-1).

The twins formation spreads the defense one way with added pressure of two spread pass receivers on one side of the formation. The right halfback will align two to three yards inside or outside of the split end and one yard off the line of scrimmage (Diagram 12-2).

The twins open formation combines the pro and the twins formation together. There is an open end to one side and a twins set to the other side. This is a very good passing and two-minute offense formation (Diagram 12-3).

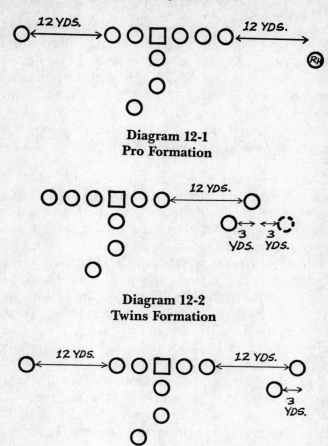

**Diagram 12-1**
**Pro Formation**

**Diagram 12-2**
**Twins Formation**

**Diagram 12-3**
**Twins Open Formation**

The double tight formation has both ends tight. A second tight end may be substituted if it will strengthen blocking. This is a good short-yardage and goal line formation.

A double open, both ends split, may also be used. This set is good for passing, to execute the triple option and to spread the defense. A second split end may be substituted or this set may be used if a team's personnel has two split end types and no tight end type.

A wing or flanker with two tight ends is another Wishbone variation. The right halfback will be a wingback one yard outside and one yard back of the right end. This gives added blocking power to the wingback side and also two quick pass receivers to one side and three total quick receivers. The flanker set is using the right halfback aligned as he does in the pro set, twelve yards outside of the right end and one yard off the line of scrimmage. The left end will be aligned tight on the flanker set.

Two slot sets can be used, a wide slot and a close slot. The wide slot is a regular Wishbone set with the split end to the right with the right halfback aligned one yard outside and one yard back of the right tackle. Note that this alignment is like the familiar Slot I used so much in all levels of offensive football today. The only difference is that the left halfback is 18 inches to the left of the fullback instead of behind the fullback. The tight slot has a split end to the left. The tight end flexes out to four feet and the right halfback aligns between the right tackle and right end one yard off the line of scrimmage. This gives added blocking strength and allows a third pass receiver to release quickly into the secondary.

All of these sets may be run from a strong formation. This is done by having the left halfback take the right halfback's alignment or becoming the man to break formation. The quarterback calls the formation and adds the word "strong" to achieve this.

## MOTION

Man in motion can be used in the same way as formations. All the formations that have been discussed can be used by using man in motion (Diagram 12-4).

Cross motioning of the opposite halfback can be used to get into strong motion sets.

Motion can be used from the broken Wishbone formations to change back into the regular Wishbone or to another broken

Wishbone formation. Diagram 12-5 shows some of these possibilities.

The fullback used as the man in motion will make the Wishbone go into a two-back split set. The fullback can go either way. Going toward the tight end side turns the formation into a split back pro set. Going toward the split end turns the formation into a split back twins set. The fullback in motion fits in well with the outside veer series described in Chapter 8. Diagram 12-6 shows the fullback in motion.

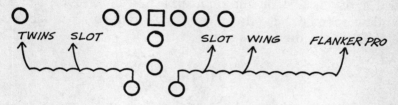

**Diagram 12-4**
**Motion into Formations**

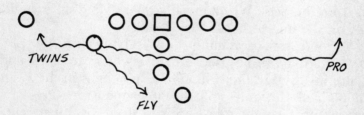

**Diagram 12-5**
**Motion from Broken Set**

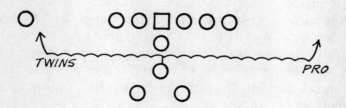

**Diagram 12-6**
**Fullback in Motion**

The quarterback's snap count must be changed slightly when man in motion is used. The snap count described in Chapter 2 is still used. All players assume their three-point stance on SET. All remain still one second. The motion man will start long motion on the quarterback's second verbal "HIKE." On long motion the quarterback draws out "READY" into "READYEEEEEEE" to allow the motion man to arrive at his desired width and calls "GO" for the ball to be snapped when the motion man is at his desired positon. The motion man can vary his speed to help in this timing. The motion man will start short motion on the quarterback's call of "READY" and time his speed to be at the desired spot on the quarterback's call of "GO" when the ball is snapped.

## SHIFTING

Shifting offensive players from one alignment to another before the snap of the ball will cause defensive problems. There are several shifts that fit well into Wishbone variations. All of the formations described earlier in the chapter can be shifted into from the basic Wishbone alignment. The shift would take place on the quarterback's "SET" call.

A good shift combining the Wishbone with the split back pro formation can be used effectively. The fullback and one end are involved in the shift. The team aligns in the Wishbone with both of the ends split (double open set). Pre-shift and quick-count Wishbone plays are run from this formation. This is an excellent formation to execute the triple option from. The fullback shifts up to a tight end position on the second verbal of "HIKE." The split end to the side that the fullback shifts to moves back one yard off the line of scrimmage and becomes a flanker back. This shift creates a split two-back pro formation. This is a type of shift to use if there are two split-end-flanker type of players on the offensive team. It is also a good shift to use if the outside veer discussed in Chapter 8 is used. Diagram 12-7 shows the shift from the Wishbone into the split back pro formation.

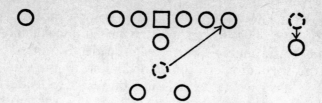

**Diagram 12-7**
**Shift from Wishbone to Split Back Pro**

A preliminary formation (the double slot) is excellent to use as a formation to shift into the Wishbone and broken bone sets. The double slot can be used with man in motion also. Some offensive plays should be run from the double slot without a shift to keep the defense honest and off balance. Diagram 12-8 shows the double slot and the Wishbone formations that can be shifted into. The end and halfbacks shift or motion into whatever formation is called by the quarterback in the huddle.

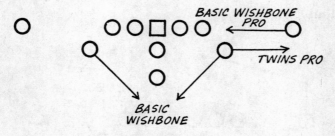

**Diagram 12-8**
**Double Slot with Shifts**

A very good trick type of play can be executed from the double slot with the correct substitution or changing of positions of properly numbered players. As the team comes out of the huddle the left halfback and the right tackle change alignments. This allows the play to be run after a shift that is not in conflict with the rules of the game. The team aligns in the double slot. They all go into a three-point stance on "SET." On "HIKE" called by the quarterback, the right tackle moves up on the line of scrimmage one yard outside the left tackle. This gives the formation an unbalanced line to the left. The left halfback stays where he aligned one yard outside the right guard. The split right end moves back one yard to become a flanker back. This shift gives the offense three quick receivers to one side of the formation with one being disguised.

All the internal linemen block in their area and pick up any charging defensive man over them. The left end releases on a post route through the safety area. The flanker releases downfield to the inside to a depth of twelve yards and screens for the right halfback. Then the flanker hooks to the inside. The right halfback goes downfield inside and times his break to the outside to run off the flanker's screen. The left halfback blocks ahead for two counts and releases into the flat. The fullback blocks the defensive end as he does on sprint out passes. The quarterback sprints to the right looking to pass to the right halfback, flanker or left halfback in that order. If no one is open, the quarterback runs the ball. Diagram 12-9 shows the double slot trick play.

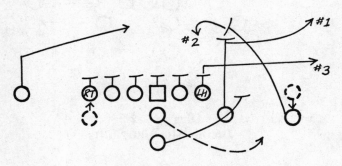

**Diagram 12-9**
**Double Slot Trick Play**

The sucker shift is designed to draw the defense offside at a critical point in the ball game. The sucker shift should be used when the offense needs five yards or less badly. This would be to get a first down on third or fourth down or to turn a passing down (long down and distance) into a run-pass down. The team substitutes a second quarterback into the game for the left halfback or will have the players align as follows. The quarterback aligns at left halfback. The fullback aligns at quarterback. The right halfback aligns at fullback. The left halfback aligns at right halfback. The offensive team aligns in the regular wishbone formation and assumes their three-point stance on the quarterback's "SET" call. On "HIKE" the backs shift into their regular positions with the left halfback shifting out into a strong twins set. The backs shift sharply to draw the defense off sides. If the defense does not jump offside, the play that is called in the huddle is executed. If it is fourth down, time out may be called and the team can re-huddle, call a punt and kick (Diagram 12-10).

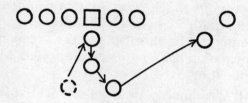

**Diagram 12-10**
**Sucker Shift**

The effectiveness of the sucker shift will diminish as scouting reports and film study pick it up. For this reason, the sucker shift should be used only when needed badly or it loses its effectiveness. The type of sucker shift may be changed from time to time to confuse different opponents.

## UNBALANCING

The basic Wishbone formation is a balanced one. This can be an advantage in recognizing defenses and being able to expect to play against a standard balanced defense. Unbalancing the line can have advantages also. They are:

1. Confuse the defense.
2. A changeup to make the opponents have to prepare for unbalancing.

3. Make the defense move their personnel to get better blocking angles.

4. The short side can be attacked quickly if the defense moves to the unbalanced side because there is less distance to go to turn the corner and be outside.

5. The long side (unbalanced side) can be attacked with an extra blocker if the defense does not move down to the unbalanced strength.

6. Advantages four and five can be used in a simple system of automatics for the quarterback. He automatics to the short side if the defense moves to the unbalanced side. He automatics to the long side if the defense does not move to the unbalanced side.

7. A very good triple option play can be executed to the short side. The basic Wishbone triple option executed to the short side of the unbalanced Wishbone formation has an outside veer effect with the fullback executing the first option.

8. All Wishbone plays can be executed from the unbalanced wishbone alignment.

The unbalanced Wishbone formation has the split end still spread and the backs in the regular Wishbone alignment. Only one tackle and the right end change alignments to allow the passing game to remain intact and effective. The tight end goes to the short side and the tackle normally on the tight end side goes over and aligns one yard outside the other tackle. This will create a strong blocking area where the two tackles align side by side (Diagram 12-11).

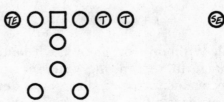

**Diagram 12-11**
**Unbalanced Wishbone**

## HALF SPREAD

A very unusual Wishbone variation is the half spread. Many Wishbone plays and other possibilities can be executed from the half spread alignment. Some of the Wishbone plays that can be executed are the veer, counter dive, quick pitch and the speed option. Passes include the sprint pass, quick screen and veer keep pass.

The half spread alignment has the center and one side of the line in regular Wishbone alignment. The halfback to the side that is in regular alignment is in his normal position. The quarterback and the fullback assume regular alignment also. The other side of the line and halfback to that side go ten to twelve yards from the center and take their regular splits. The halfback lines up two yards deep in the guard-tackle gap.

One special play is having the center snap the ball sideways to the flanked halfback. The halfback receives the snap and runs to the outside. The flanked end and tackle block to the inside. The flanked guard observes the defensive alignment and blocks accordingly. His first rule is to pull and block the first man aligned outside the end's block. If no man is aligned outside the end's block, the guard pulls upfield to block. If no defensive man is outside the end either on or off the line of scrimmage the guard will block to the inside. The regular

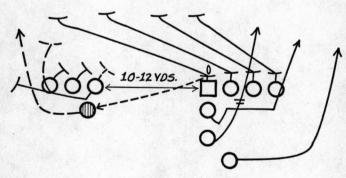

**Diagram 12-12**
**Half Spread Center Throwout Play**

linemen block for two counts with a base block and then release downfield to block. The quarterback, fullback and onside halfback fake a Veer play to the right (Diagram 12-12).

The installation and use of Wishbone variations should be controlled. Variations should only be installed to benefit the team and help it have an advantage over the defense. Only variations that the team can master should be considered. There should not be a lot of variations just to appear fancy. Have a purpose for each variation.

# CHAPTER *13*

# *Beating the Clock with the Wishbone*

The good football team must know how to deal with the clock. The players must know when the clock starts and stops on different types of situations. The team must know how to keep the clock running and how to stop the clock.

## KILL THE CLOCK PLAY

This is a play to allow the team extra precious seconds to run off the clock when the team wants to use up as much time as possible, keep the clock running and not get a penalty for too much time.

Most teams will just come out of the huddle and snap the ball to the quarterback and he immediately falls to the ground over the football. Time is not used up to a maximum this way. The idea to take as much time as possible before the snap comes from Homer Rice in his excellent book *Triple Option Football*. Don't huddle to kill the clock. Align over the football by the time the official places it down ready for play. All players align in a two-point stance. The quarterback starts counting on placement of the ball by the official. The quarterback counts in reverse from twenty-five (25) down to five (5). He watches the clock and uses it to make his count down. After reaching the

**207**

count of five, the quarterback starts his regular snap count of SET, HIKE, READY, GO. The football will be snapped on GO. In using this procedure, the maximum 25 seconds are used before the snap and a penalty will not occur for taking too much time before the snap of the ball. Also, the official cannot make a mistake in his timing for the 25 seconds allowed before the snap of the ball. Pressure is put on the official to be correct in his timing.

The kill the clock play has all the linemen wedge block to the inside using the center as the apex to the wedge. The quarterback takes the snap, reverses out as he does on the power plays and steps back into the cup formed by the three deep backs. Then he chop steps as long as possible. The quarterback will drop to the ground over the ball just before being hit by the opposition. The fullback takes a short jab step to the right to allow the quarterback to come by him. Then he comes to the left and blocks the first opponent to show up the middle. Each of the halfbacks takes a step up and forms a second wedge with the fullback and blocks the first opponent to show on their respective sides. The backs let their opponents come to them. They do not leave each other and break their wedge. This kill the clock play uses the maximum amount of time before the snap of the ball and the maximum amount of time after the snap of the ball. This procedure and play will use several more seconds off the clock than any other type of kill the clock play. The Wishbone formation is the best formation to use the kill the clock play described because of the close alignment of the three deep backs. Diagram 13-1 shows the kill the clock play.

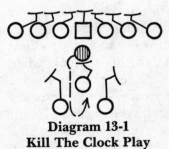

**Diagram 13-1**
**Kill The Clock Play**

## TWO-MINUTE OFFENSE

This is the type of offensive play that is required when the team is behind late in either half, especially the second half. There are some rules affecting the stopping and starting of the clock that every player should know. Do not huddle unless the ball is dead and the clock is stopped. Have a quick huddle on any stoppage of the clock. Hustle to the line of scrimmage and be ready to run the play by the time the clock starts. Runners and receivers should know when to get out of bounds to stop the clock. The quarterback must be able to get to an official quickly to call timeout after a play is run. The quarterback must also know how to throw a pass out of bounds to stop the clock.

The two-minute offense must be practiced over and over to be effective. The game plan will determine the formations and the best plays to use in the two-minute offense. The game plan, plays that have been successful in the game, score, weather, field conditions and defense will determine the best play to call.

A wide-out formation to spread the defense and to pass more effectively from is best to use. The pro, twins or twins open formations are preferred (Diagram 13-2).

The plays selected should have a good chance for long gainers. Running plays should include the option, triple option, trap, draw and reverse. The individual player assignments for each of these plays have already been described earlier. Diagrams 13-3 through 13-7 show these two-minute offensive plays.

Pass plays should include a screen, flood, throwback, bend, reverse pass and a quick pass to throw the ball out of bounds to stop the clock. Diagrams 13-8 through 13-13 show these two-minute offensive pass plays.

The procedure used to call a play at the line of scrimmage in the two-minute offense, when a huddle is not used, is the same as changing a play at the line of scrimmage using automatics. This is a time-saving procedure and cuts down on the chance of mistakes since one learning procedure can be used in two game situations.

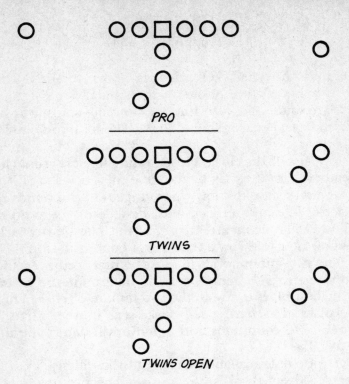

**Diagram 13-2**
**Two-Minute Offense Formations**

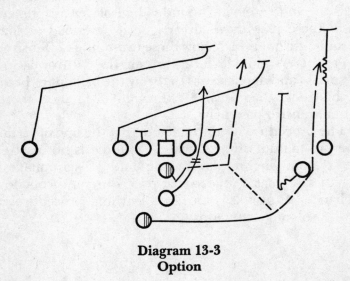

**Diagram 13-3**
**Option**

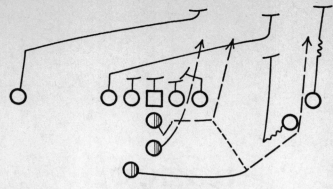

**Diagram 13-4**
**Triple Option**

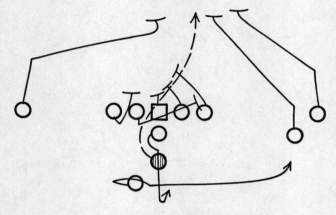

**Diagram 13-5**
**Trap**

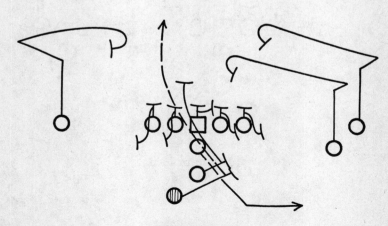

**Diagram 13-6**
**Draw**

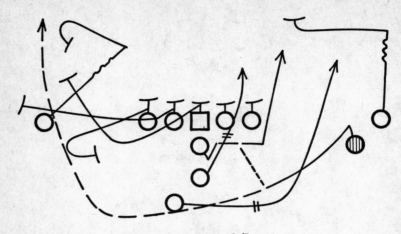

**Diagram 13-7**
**Reverse**

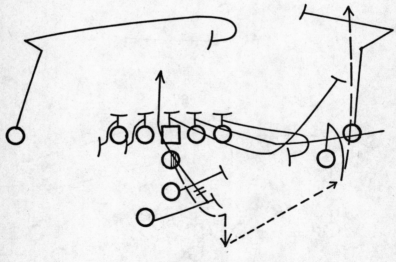

**Diagram 13-8**
**Screen**

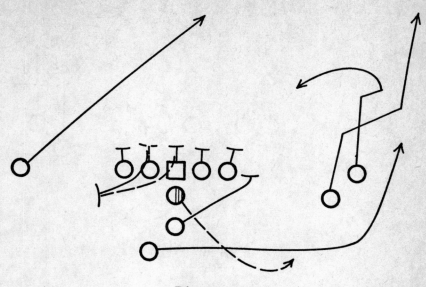

**Diagram 13-9**
**Flood**

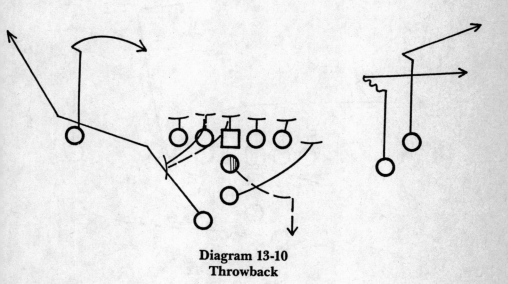

**Diagram 13-10**
**Throwback**

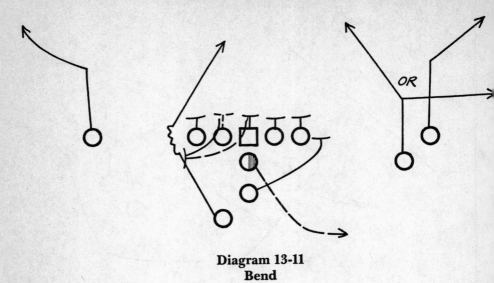

**Diagram 13-11**
**Bend**

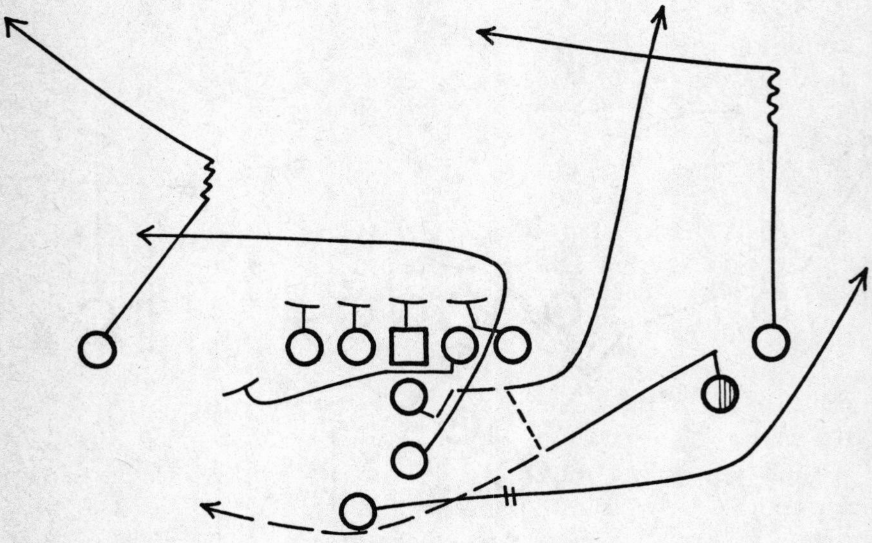

**Diagram 13-12**
**Reverse Pass**

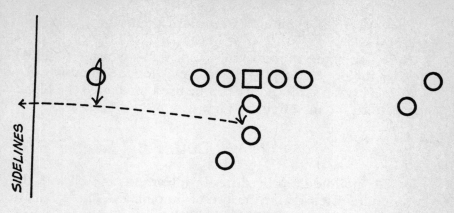

**Diagram 13-13**
**Quick Pass to Stop the Clock**

## AUTOMATICS

The following rules govern the use of automatics or changing the play at the line of scrimmage. These same rules apply in the two-minute offense and the no-huddle offense.

1. The quarter being played is the "live" number. Call it before calling the play. Any other number called except the "live" quarter number will be a dummy call. Several of these should be made during the course of the game.

2. Do not use the quarter number in the two-minute offense. Just call the play. The quarter number is not needed in the no-huddle offense.

3. The quarterback glances from left to right across the defense and if he sees that the play called is not desired against the defense he may change the play that is called in the huddle.

4. To change the play, the quarterback calls the quarter number that is being played and then the desired play. He only uses the first letter of the play word and the number. An example would be V two for Veer Two.

5. Keep the same snap count that is called in the huddle.

6. All the two-minute offense and the no-huddle offense are on Go.

7. Use some dummy calls. Call some quarter numbers besides the one being played and a play for the dummy call.

8. This same procedure can be used to change the blocking pattern on any offensive play.

## NO HUDDLE

The no-huddle procedure for a team fits in well with the two-minute offense and the use of automatics. The offensive team may gain several advantages by using a no-huddle procedure in their offensive game plan. These advantages are:

1. The tempo of the game can be changed if it is to the offensive team's advantage.

2. The element of surprise can help the offense.

3. The psychology involved helps the offense.

4. The no huddle cuts down on the time allowed the defense to call their defenses. This can limit the defense to one basic defense and cut down on the number of alignments and stunts allowed.

# INDEX

# INDEX

**219**